GCSE Python
A Guide to the Practical Component

GCSE Python will introduce students to programming in python, using a practical approach. The book is geared towards anyone wanting to learn how to program in python, and especially students studying computing at Key Stage 4.

Patrick Dawkins

GCSE Python: A Guide to the Practical Component
By Patrick Dawkins

First Edition Published 2013.

Editor: Carolette Fullerton

Copyright © 2013, Patrick O. Dawkins

E-Mail: pdawkins@gcsepython.com

All rights reserved, No part of this publication may be reproduced or transmitted in any form or by any means, electronic or mechanical, including photocopying, scanning, recording, or any information storage and retrieval system, without permission in writing from the author.

ISBN: 978 – 1 – 291 – 44394 – 3

About the Author

Patrick Dawkins is a qualified teacher with more than ten years teaching experience. He read for the B.Sc. in Computer Science and Mathematics. He obtained the qualified teacher status (QTS) at Brunel University: England. He lectured Computer Science and Mathematics at a teacher training institution for two years. He has served as an examiner for Mathematics and Computer Science. He now teaches GCSE and GCE ICT, GCSE Computer Science and GCE Mathematics. While not teaching, Patrick enjoys reading, exercising and watching Criminal Minds.

Join the discussion @pdawkins

Key to conventions used in this book

1) Program Code that can be interpreted → `Font name: Courier New`
   Example: `print("This code can be interpreted")`

2) Place holder normally for variables → `<Angle bracket>`
   Example: `len(<string_name>)`

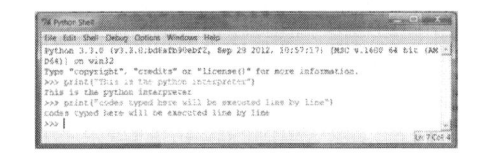

3)

This is the python interpreter. Codes typed here will be interpreted

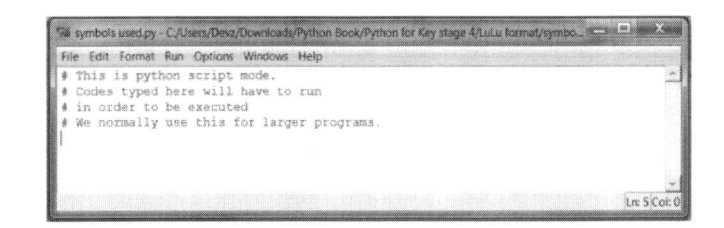

4)

This is the script mode. Codes written in this mode will have to run in order to be executed. We normally use this for larger programs. Notice that there are no chevrons in the left hand margin.

Introduction

The central notion of computer science is that of an algorithm. Algorithms are unambiguous executable steps that terminate in a finite time. In computer science we study these algorithms and implement them using various programming languages.

This book will focus on developing programming skills and implementing these in a popular and powerful programming language called python. The book is written for students pursuing the GCSE computer science course. The concepts are explained followed by specific syntax, followed by examples. The interpreter is used throughout to give students real hands on experience. There are extensive practice exercises at the end of each chapter that is designed to test what have been covered in each chapter. The practice exercise will have a mixture of easy to difficult questions with majority of the questions designed to test students' thinking skills.

The worked solution is a control assessment type that is designed to give students experiences in developing a larger solution. The source code will be available for download from the web site.

Each chapter is summarised in videos as a playlist on my YouTube channel, please subscribe to access all the videos for free. The idea is to use the videos to supplement the in depth theory, and not to substitute for the book.

http://www.youtube.com/user/syringe876.

Play list - http://www.youtube.com/user/syringe876/videos?flow=grid&view=1

The companion site for **GCSE Python: A Guide to the Practical Component** is http://www.gcsepython.com . You will find downloadable source code, and other teaching supporting materials.

Comments and feedback to pdawkins@gcsepython.com

To the teacher

The following use of this book is highly recommended. The idea is to implement a "flipped classroom", where teachers can use technology (book and video in this case) to allow students to be familiar with key concepts before lesson which will give teacher the opportunity to interact more with students in the classroom and solve more difficult problems.

1) The teacher should give students access to chapter notes, examples and explanation before the lesson.

2) The students should read, practice and watch the companion videos before the lesson.

3) The teacher should guide the students through solving the practice exercises that are at the end of each chapter. These should be done during the lesson and possibly changing the solution for deeper understanding.

The worked example was deliberately written to use most of the concepts covered in the book, and draws heavily on the use of data structure (class and List), for a working solution. Teachers can really differentiate by outcome, by focussing on how students use functions, variables, error handling procedures, classes and other data structures. The control assessments have similar structure.

Teachers should allow students to refer to and use this book in preparation for the control assessment as there is a natural build up to this.

To the Student

You are encouraged to read each chapter, type and run the examples in the chapters, to aid your understanding.

Watch the videos on the companion website.

Attempt the end of chapter practice exercise to the best of your ability.

The worked example in Chapter 10 was deliberately written to use most of the concepts covered in the book, and draws heavily on the use of data structure (class and List), for a working solution. Your control assessments have similar structure.

Use this book in preparation for your control assessment as there is a natural build up to this.

Contents

Chapter 0: Computer Science and Python 11
    0.1   Definitions 12
    0.2   Expressing Algorithms 16
    0.2.1   Pseudo-code 16
    0.2.2   Comment Statements 17
    0.2.3   Sequencing 18
    0.2.4   Assignment Statement 18
    0.2.5   Input Statements 19
    0.2.5   Output Statements 20
    0.2.6   Selection or Conditional Statements 21
    0.2.7   Repetition or Looping Statements 22
    0.2.8   Functions and Procedures 23
    0.2.9   Flowcharts 25
    Practice Exercise 0 27

Chapter 1: Numbers and Operations 28
    1.1   Let's write our first program 29
    1.2   Order of operation 30
    PRACTICE EXERCISE 1 31

Chapter 2: Values, Variables and Expressions 32
    2.1   Definitions 33
    2.2   Multiple Assignments 35
    PRACTICE EXERCISE 2 36

Chapter 3: Data Types 38
    3.0   Data types in python 39
    3.1   Integers 39
    3.2   Floating Point Number 40
    3.3   Strings 41
    3.3.1   Assigning String to a Variable 41
    3.4   Other string operations 43
    3.4.1   Sub-sequence 43

3.4.2	Finding string within string	44
3.4.3	Finding the length of a string	44
3.5	Upper case character	44
3.5.1	Lower case character	45
3.5.2	Concatenate String (+)	45
3.6	Testing for membership using the in operator	46
3.7	Converting Data type	46
3.8	Taking input from the user	48
	Practice Exercise 3	49

Chapter 4 : Functions 50

4.1	Definition	51
4.1.1	Why do we use functions?	51
4.1.2	Function Syntax	51
4.1.3	Returning values	52
4.2	Parameters and Arguments	52
4.4	Program Flow	55
	PRACTICE EXERCISE 4	56

CHAPTER 5 : CONTROL STRUCTURES 57

5.1	Selection or Conditional Statements	58
5.1.1	IF Statement	58
5.1.2	IF ELSE Statement	59
5.2	Loops	60
5.2.1	For Loop	60
5.2.2	The range function	61
5.3.1	While Loop	62
5.3.2	Break	63
	Practise Exercise 5	65

CHAPTER 6 : LIST 67

6.1	Definition	68
6.1.1	Selecting individual elements	68
6.2	List operations	69
6.3.1	Selecting a sub-sequence in the list – Slicing	69
6.4	Editing a list	70

6.5	List of List	70
6.6	List methods	71
6.7	List Methods	75
	Practice Exercise 6	77

Chapter 7 : Dictionary ... 79

7.1	Definition	80
7.2	Modifying values in a dictionary	80
7.2.1	Deleting Entries	81
7.3	List of keys and values	81
	Practice Exercise 7	82

Chapter 8 : Working With Files ... 83

8.1	Writing to a file	85
8.2	Printing a file to the screen	86
8.3	Appending a file	87
8.4	File Path	88
8.5	Working with Databases	89
8.6	SQL	90
8.6.1	The CREATE TABLE Statement	90
8.6.2	The SELECT Statement	91
8.6	The WHERE Clause	92
8.6.4	The UPDATE Statement	93
8.6.5	The DELETE Statement	94
8.6.6	The INSERT INTO Statement	95
8.7	SQL and Python	96
	Practice Exercise 8	100

Chapter 9 : Classes ... 103

9.1	Object Oriented Programming (OOP)	104
9.2	Why do we use classes?	105
9.3	Data types in Python	106
9.4	Defining a class	107
9.4.1	Using the class	109
	Practice Exercise 9	110

Chapter 10: Dealing With Errors 111

    10.1   Exceptions and errors 112

    10.2   Syntax error 113

    10.3   Runtime Errors 115

    10.4   Semantic or logical Error 117

    10.5   Dealing with errors 118

        10.5.1   The try statement 118

        10.5.2   The try statement with multiple exceptions 119

        10.5.3   The optional else clause 120

        10.5.4   The try – finally statement 120

    Practice Exercise 10 122

Worked Solution 123

Quick How To 132

Glossary 133

References 136

Chapter 0: Computer Science and Python

What we will learn:
- About Computer Science
- Algorithm
- High-level and low-level languages
- Compilers and Interpreters

Keywords
- Computer Science
- Programming
- Algorithm
- Python
- Compilers,
- Interpreters

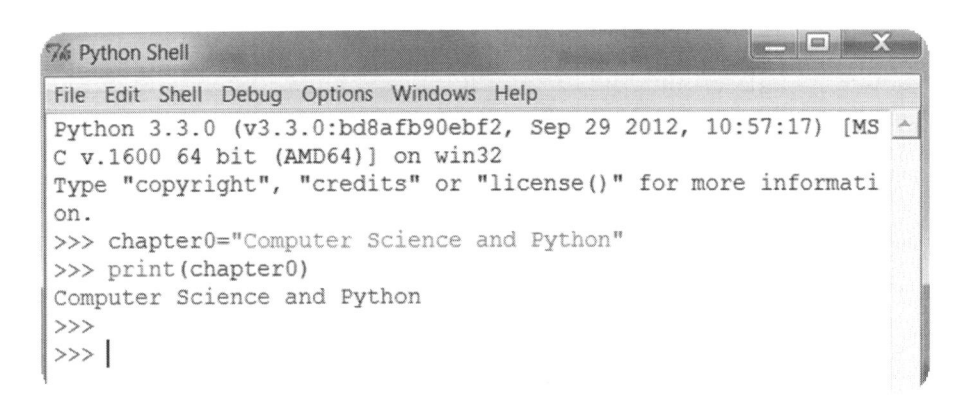

```
Python 3.3.0 (v3.3.0:bd8afb90ebf2, Sep 29 2012, 10:57:17) [MSC v.1600 64 bit (AMD64)] on win32
Type "copyright", "credits" or "license()" for more information.
>>> chapter0="Computer Science and Python"
>>> print(chapter0)
Computer Science and Python
>>>
>>>
```

Subject Content	Learning Outcomes
3.1.3 Program Flow Control • Sequencing • Selection • Iteration	• Understand how programs can be broken down into smaller problems and how these steps can be represented by the use of devices such s flowcharts and structure diagrams
3.1.9 Algorithms	• Understand that algorithms are computational solutions that always finish and return an answer • Be able to create algorithms to solve simple problems

0.1 Definitions

Computer Science is the study of the design of algorithms, their properties, linguistic and mechanical realisation.

Algorithm is a collection of unambiguous and executable operations to perform some task in a finite amount of time.

Computer scientists are therefore concerned with designing computer programs to solve problems. Although computers are fairly recent in the form we know them (the first computer was built some 60 years ago), computer science can trace its roots back to a long way before that. Both the idea of algorithm and the idea of building some mechanical device to execute these date back to some 1500 years. The single most important skill that a computer scientist must possess is problem solving skill. The idea of a problem having multiple solutions is prevalent throughout this text. With this in mind it is therefore vital for the computer scientist to be able to assess and compare solutions and choose an optimal solution. In addition to thinking about a solution this text is concerned with expressing and implementing the solution in python code.

Computer programming is an interesting way of creating instructions for a computer to interpret and produces results for the users.

These instructions can be written using programming languages such as C, C++, Java and Python. This book will focus on programming in Python.

What is python?

Python is an interpreted general purpose programming language which conforms to multiple ways of programming called **programming paradigms**. Languages that support multiple programming paradigms are called hybrid languages.

Python is an interpreted language. Python can operate in two modes namely **interactive mode** and a **script mode**. We typically use the interactive mode to test and debug small amount of code, and the script mode for running larger projects.

Downloading and Installing Python

Python is an open-source programming language and is therefore free to use. You can download python from http://www.python.org/download/ . In this book we will be using version 3.3.0.

Once you have installed the correct version of python, you can start the IDLE python GUI. Figure 1 show what the interpreter should look like.

Figure 1

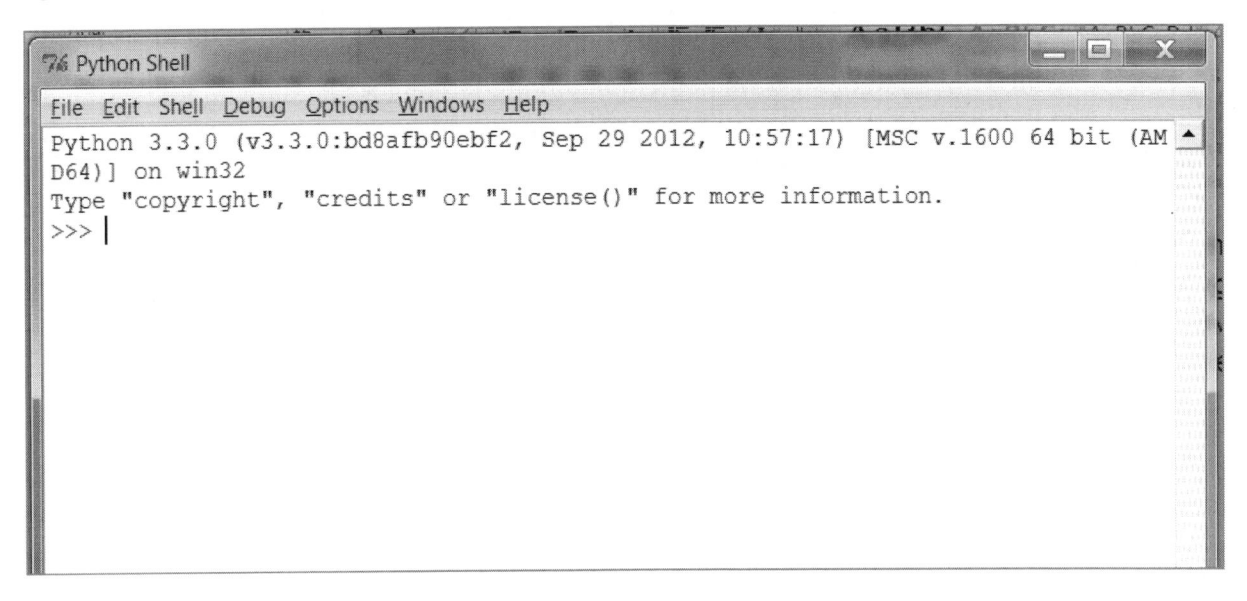

```
Python 3.3.0 (v3.3.0:bd8afb90ebf2, Sep 29 2012, 10:57:17) [MSC v.1600 64 bit (AMD64)] on win32
Type "copyright", "credits" or "license()" for more information.
>>>
```

Low-Level vs. High-level Language

Python is a **high-level** language. High-level languages are written using codes that are similar to human read language for example we use statements such as `print()`, `input()`, to print and take input from the user respectively. One could perhaps guess what these statements do without even seeing these in action.

There are also low-level languages, these are also known as machine language. Typically computer only understand low-level language (machine language) and therefore all high-level language will have to be translated to a machine language before they can be executed. *Table 1* below gives a full comparison between these two languages.

Table 1

Low-Level Language	High-Level language
No conversion needed since the computer understand machine language naturally as a result code will execute faster.	Codes have to be converted to machine language and therefore take a longer time for this conversion
Much more difficult to read and understand by other programmers as all instructions have to be written in machine code.	Easier to understand as keywords used are closely aligned to everyday language
Very specific to the computer that the program is written for.	Programs are portable seen that the language abstract away from the underlying computer and CPU.
Only support primitive data types understood by the computer.	Support a wider range of data types, giving the functionality where the user can define his own data type.

There are two methods of exaction available to the programmer, namely compiling and interpreting.

Compiler vs. Interpreter

A programming language is interpreted if the source code goes directly to an executable format, however with a compiled language such as C, an intermediary file is created called an object code, which is then executed.

The instructions that are written in python or any other programming language are called program code. Compilers then create object code or byte codes of the entire program, which is them executed by the computer. On the other hand interpreters take each line, translate and execute the translated line, before turning its attention to the other line.

Figure 2

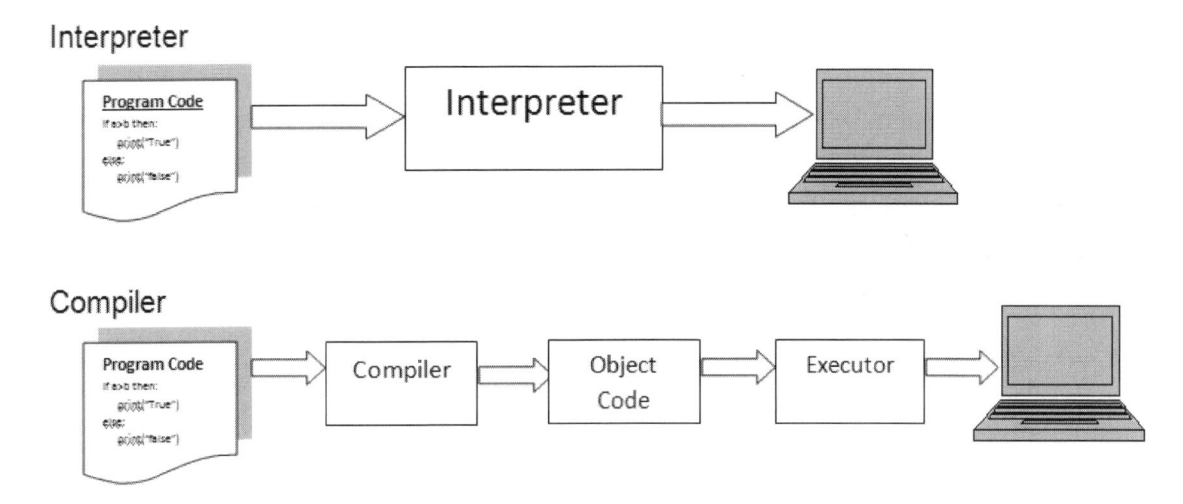

Interpreter

Compiler

There are clear trade-offs with using compilers and interpreters. Compiled codes are always faster to execute, there are two reasons for this; firstly, the compiler does all the translation and execution at once. Since all the translation is done during compilation, there is no need to do this during execution and therefore the compiled code is executed faster. With the interpreters each line is translated before execution; the interpreter interleaves, translate and then execute the codes. Secondly seen that the entire program is examined during compilation, the compiler has the ability to look at the entire program and find opportunities for optimisation. Whether by using less processing power by finding a more efficient method for carrying out a computation or by using less resources. The interpreter however, executes one line at a time and therefore uses more resources and processing time.

Interpreted programs are easier to debug. Quite often one writes a program that is syntactically correct, but produces a different output when executed. With a compiler sometimes it is virtually impossible to stop a program in the middle of execution to examine the state of the program, where as with an interpreter it is often easy to do this. After all an interpreter translate and execute each line and therefore you can stop execution after each line. Fortunately, compilers are now being developed with the facility called **steppers**. Steppers are used to stop programs in the middle of execution and debug (look for errors) them; these are becoming increasingly available with both interpreters and compilers.

0.2   Expressing Algorithms

The first step in programming is the design of an algorithm to solve the problem under consideration. Algorithms are abstract specification of the intended solution. They are independent of any programming language. In this section we will examine two methods of specifying algorithms, namely pseudo-code and flowcharts.

0.2.1   Pseudo-code

Pseudo-code is a stylized form of English. It is a compound word broken down as Pseudo which means false and code, to highlight the fact that it is not specific to any language and therefore cannot be compiled and executed on the computer. Pseudo-code forms the bridge between natural language and compiled code.

In pseudo-code instructions are generally specified using one of the following constructs:

- Comment Statements
- Sequencing
- Assignment Statement
- Input / Output
- Selection or conditional statement
- Repetition or looping statements
- Functions and Procedures

Selection and repetition are referred to as control construct as they affect the normal sequence of the pseudo-code.

Before we examine the constructs used in pseudo-code we'll turn our attention to a very key concept called variables. Variables can be considered as a storage area for some value, similar to a shoe box that stores a shoe. For our purpose a variable is a location in the computer's memory that holds some data. There are two sides to a variable, namely the storage location and the value that is stored at this location. Because computer memory is located by using memory address variables location is often referred to as variable address. There are several reasons for wanting to use variables in a computer program. We'll discuss three of the most prominent reasons below.

Why do we use variables	Example
1) To temporarily store the value of some result in our algorithm.	If we want to find the average of three numbers, we can temporarily store the sum of the three numbers before dividing by three.
2) To store input for the user	If we want the user to enter the numbers to find the average of, then we can store these numbers in a variable.
3) To keep track of some information during the algorithm	We want the user to enter many numbers then enter a dummy value (say -1) in the end, we would want to keep track of how many numbers were entered.

We will return to variables in python in chapter 2. Now that we understand the concept of variables and how they are used in an algorithm we return to constructs in pseudo-code.

0.2.2 Comment Statements

Syntax:
```
# comment text
```

Comments are used to include normal English in your pseudo-code. They always start the line with the hash symbol, and can span multiple lines. Comments can also be used at the end of a line beside other pseudo-code constructs. We typically use comments for two reasons:

1) Using a top-down refinement model, the full solution can be defined using pseudo-code; it can then be translated to other pseudo-code constructs.

2) To explain why a particular statement is used in the solution. Recall that using pseudo-code is the first step in programming a solution, quite of the person that write the pseudo-code is different to the person that translate this into a computer program. Comments make it easier for the programmer to translate this and avoid errors.

Examples:
```
# We first initialize our counter to zero
```

0.2.3 Sequencing

Sequencing means putting one pseudo-code statement after another. This is important as we quite often require an algorithm to do more than one thing, the order in which these tasks are carried out is important and will affect our solution. A pseudo-code will be interpreted from top to bottom, unless directed by some control construct. We will see sequencing used throughout.

0.2.4 Assignment Statement

Syntax:
```
<var> ← <exp>
```

Where `<var>` is a name of a variable and `<exp>` is a valid expression. This is read as variable is assigned to the expression. The expression on the right is computed and the value is then assigned to the variable on the right.

Examples:
```
name ← Benjamin
age ← 23
total ← sub_total + vat_amount
```

In some solutions there is a need to store collection of data, one way of storing this collection is using so called array. An array is a collection of data items of the same type that is accessible by using the same name and an index for each element. The assignment statement is also used to store values in arrays.

Syntax for assigning values to an array:
```
<var>[index] ← <exp>
```

Where `<var>` is a name of the one dimensional array and `index` is a valid integer value to represent the position and `<exp>` is the value to be stored in the array at position `index`.

Example:
```
Sales[3] ← 15000        #Wednesdays' sale figure
```

Syntax for assigning values to a two-dimensional array:

```
<var>[index1][index2] ← <exp>
```

Example:
```
Coach[3][8] ← 5      #The eight row in coach 3
```

In the example above 5 is stored in eight index in the array found at position 3.

Syntax for initializing array of n values:
```
<var> ← [<exp1>, <exp2>, ..., <expn>]
```

Example:
```
Days ← [Mon, Tue, Wed, Thur, Fri]
```

In the example Days will have the values `[Mon, Tue, Wed, Thur, Fri]`

0.2.5 Input Statements

Input statements are used to get additional information. This can be from the user or reading from a file. Users normally enter data by typing on the keyboard, however with the advent of touch screen and more advance graphical user interface this input can come from a variety of source. Luckily the source is irrelevant for our pseudo-code; we only differentiate between input entered by the user and input read from a file. Both methods are represented below.

Syntax - User:
```
USERINPUT
```

Example:
```
score ← USERINPUT
```

Here the program will pause and wait for the user to enter some input, then store this input in the variable score.

Syntax - File:
```
READLINE( file, n)
```

Example:
```
month2 ← READLINE(month.txt, 2)
```

If the contents of the file `month.txt` is:
```
1 January
2 February
3 March
4 April
```

Then `month2` will be assigned `2 February`.

0.2.5 Output Statements

Output statements are used to either display values on the screen or write values to a file.

Syntax - Screen:
```
OUTPUT value
```

Example:
```
OUTPUT message
OUTPUT "Pseudo-code is fun"
```

Here we distinguish between literal and variables; whenever we use speech mark the text between the speech marks will be displayed on the screen, to print the value that is stored in a variable we use the name of the variable only without speech marks.

Syntax - File:
```
WRITELINE( file, n, value)
```

Example:
```
WRITELINE( month.txt, 5, "5 May")
```

From the example file above will result in:

1 January
2 February
3 March
4 April
5 May

0.2.6   Selection or Conditional Statements

Selection or conditional statements perform some command based on the result of some test.

Syntax :
```
IF <test> THEN
     <true Statement>
ELSE
     <false statement>
ENDIF
```

Example:
```
IF score > 50 THEN
    OUTPUT "Pass"
ELSE
    OUTPUT "Fail"
ENDIF
```

Here we test if the score is greater than 50 and print a message based on the result. Note that only one of the commands will be carried out, as the test can only be true or false.

There is another version of this selection where the ELSE clause is optional, we'll discuss an example below.

```
IF value = 7 THEN
    OUTPUT "Found"
ENDIF
```

In this version the statement is only executed of the test is true and is skipped otherwise.

We can also use a multiple selection statement
Syntax :
```
CASE <exp> OF
    <exp1>: <statements>
    <exp2>: <statements>
    ...
    <expn>: <statements>
ELSE
    <statements>
ENDCASE
```

Example:
```
CASE choice OF
     1: Add_Student()
     2: Print_List()
     3: Edit_Details()
     4: Delete_Student()
     0: Exit
ELSE
     OUTPUT "Please re-enter"
ENDCASE
```

Where Add_Student(), Print_List(), Edit_Details(), Delete_Student() are procedures. Porcedure and Functions are discussed below. This can be used to go to section of the program based on the user selection (value stored in choice).

0.2.7 Repetition or Looping Statements

Sometimes we want to perform the same task a number of times, for example we may want to calculate ten percent discount on all items on sale, or print a message to the screen five times. It turns out that we have three options available namely the WHILE loop, FOR loop and REPEAT loop. We will discuss these below.

Syntax - WHILE:
```
     WHILE <condition>
          <statements>
     ENDWHILE
```

Example:
```
number ← 1
WHILE number<15
     OUTPUT number
     number ← number+1
```

The condition is tested at the beginning of the loop, if the condition is true then the command is performed. It is important that there is some statement within the while loop, that makes the condition false. In the example above the statement `number ← number+1` ensure that number will be equal to or greater than 15.

Syntax - FOR:
```
     FOR <var> ← <start> TO <stop>
          <statements>
     ENDFOR
```

Example:
```
FOR   number← 1 TO 20
      OUTPUT number
ENDFOR
```

Will result in printing the numbers from 1 to 20. The variable is assigned to the starting value and increment by one up to the stop value.

Syntax - REPEAT:
```
REPEAT
      <statements>
UNTIL <condition>
```

Example:
```
REPEAT
      OUTPUT "Guess the magic number"
      guess ← USERINPUT
UNTIL guess =7
```

The statements will be repeated until the condition becomes true. Note that with this control structure the statement will be executed at least once, seen that the condition is at the end of the loop.

0.2.8 Functions and Procedures

Sometimes in our algorithm we want to include a calculation at different points in the algorithm. This is often used to reduce complexity in the code. Consider the situation where we want to find the average mark for a group of students where each student has three individual score. We could define a function or a procedure to do this.

Syntax - Function:
```
FUNCTION name(<parm_List>)
      <statements>
ENDFUNCTION
```

Example:
```
FUNCTION larger(a,b)
     IF a>b THEN
           value ← a
     ELSE
           value ← b
     ENDIF
     RETURN value
ENDFUNCTION
```

Here we make the distinction between a function and a procedure. It turns out that a function will return a value whereas as procedure will not.

The scope of the parameter (a and b) in this case is only valid within the function.

The parameter list can be empty.

Below we define a procedure.

```
PROCEDURE greetings(name)
    OUTPUT "Hello"
    OUTPUT name
    OUTPUT "Pseudo-code is fun"
ENDPROCEDURE
```

Notice here that the procedure will print the greetings with a given name.

We can use a function or a procedure in our pseudo-code by calling it and supplying the correct parameter (input) and assigning the return value from a function to a suitable variable. The main advantages of using functions and procedures are:

Advantages of using functions and procedures
1) Many developers can work on the same problem by using different function call
2) They promote algorithm re-use and help with maintaining the solution
3) Promote divide and conquer where the big task is broken down in small chunk and solved

0.2.9 Flowcharts

The second method available to us to specify algorithm is the use of flowcharts. A flowchart is a pictorial representation of an algorithm that uses geometric figures to represent the different constructs and flow lines to show how these are linked together. The table below summarises the figures that are use and their meaning.

Symbol	Meaning & Use
(rounded rectangle)	Start / Stop Symbol – Used to show the beginning and the end of a flowchart
(rectangle)	Process Symbol – used to show any command that the computer needs to execute except decisions.
(parallelogram)	Input / Output Symbol – This is used to take input from the user or from a file, and to send output from the algorithm, whether to the screen or writing to a file. The information in this symbol should be clear about the intended use.
(diamond)	Decision Symbol – Used to show that the computer need to make a decision, and the path taken should be based on the decision. The condition should be included in the box, and the path leaving the box clearly labelled.
(rectangle with double vertical lines)	Procedure Symbol – Used to show that we are using a procedure that is defined at some other section in our algorithm, or a built in procedure
(circles labelled A)	Join Symbol – Used to show that this section of a flowchart is connected to another section with the same name. This is used when flowcharts take up more than one page.
→	Flow Line – use to show the direction of flow, the arrow head indicate the direction.

Example:

The following flowchart will ask the user to enter two numbers and print the larger number to the screen.

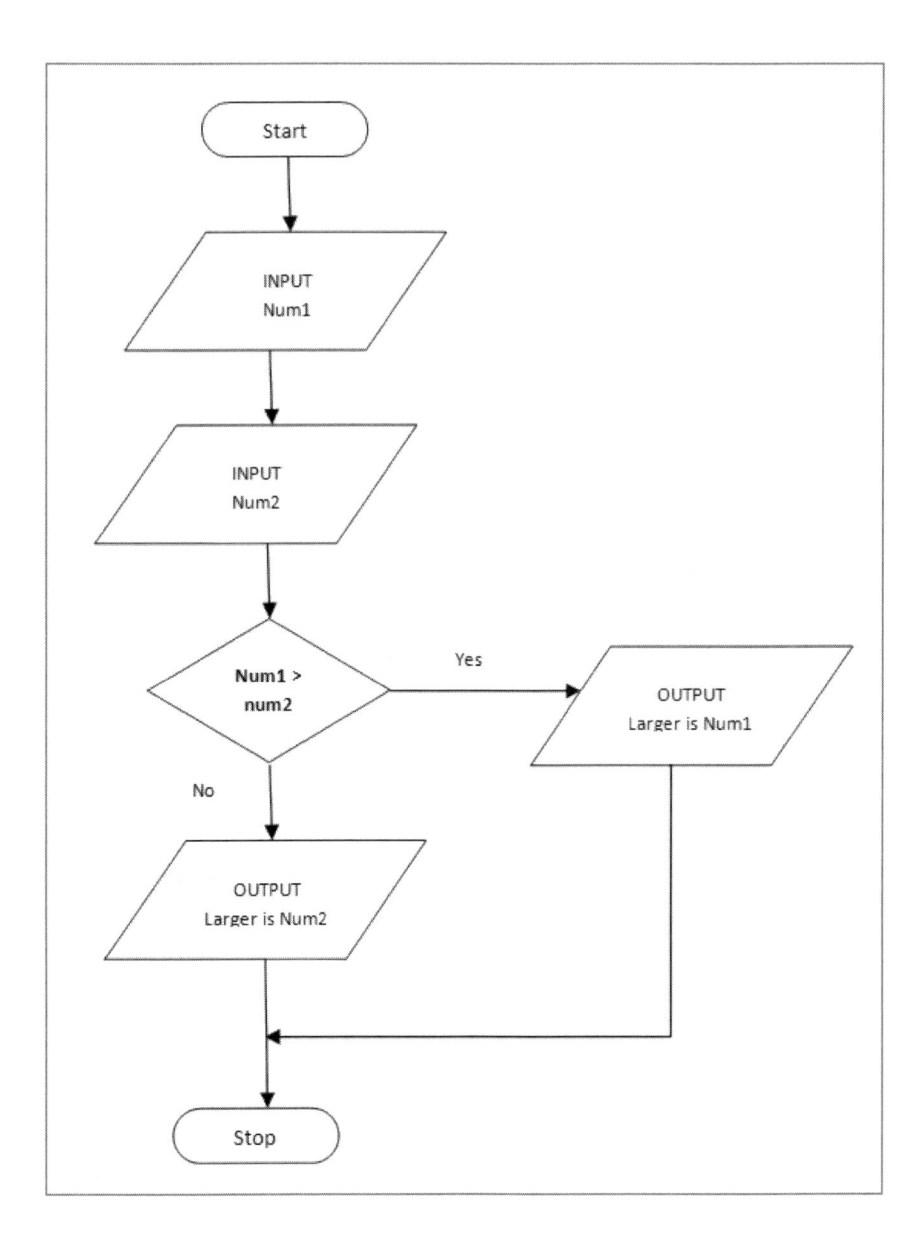

```
                    ┌─────────┐
                    │  Start  │
                    └────┬────┘
                         ↓
                   ╱─────────╲
                  ╱   INPUT    ╲
                  ╲   Num1     ╱
                   ╲─────────╱
                         ↓
                   ╱─────────╲
                  ╱   INPUT    ╲
                  ╲   Num2     ╱
                   ╲─────────╱
                         ↓
                      ╱╲
                     ╱  ╲          Yes      ╱─────────────╲
                    ╱Num1>╲─────────────→  ╱   OUTPUT      ╲
                    ╲num2 ╱                ╲ Larger is Num1╱
                     ╲  ╱                   ╲─────────────╱
                      ╲╱                           │
                       │ No                        │
                       ↓                           │
                 ╱─────────────╲                   │
                ╱   OUTPUT      ╲                  │
                ╲ Larger is Num2╱                  │
                 ╲─────────────╱                   │
                       │                           │
                       ↓←──────────────────────────┘
                    ┌─────────┐
                    │  Stop   │
                    └─────────┘
```

It should become clear that using flowchart is not the best method to express long algorithms, and for this reason pseudo-code is more widely used than flowcharts.

Practice Exercise 0

1) Download and install python.

2) What is computer science?

3) What is the difference between a compiler and an interpreter?

4) What are the advantages and disadvantages of using a compiler?

5) What are the advantages and disadvantages of using an interpreter?

6) The central notion of computer science is that of an algorithm. Explain what an algorithm is?

7) What are the two modes that python can operate in?

8) Python is a high-level language. How does high-level language differ from low-level language?

9) What do programmers use steppers for?

10) What is the difference between programming and debugging?

11) Write pseudo-code for a program that prompts the user for five numbers, between 0 and 100 inclusive. The program should then find the average, and print it on the screen.

12) Write a pseudo-code to calculate the area of a circle. The program should prompt the user to enter the radius of a circle. The value of PI is 3.14. The area is calculated as PI * radius*radius.

13) Write a program that asks the user his / her name, the program should then say "Hello <name>, Have a good day".

14) Create flowcharts for questions 11 – 13 above

Chapter 1: Numbers and Operations

What we will learn:
- Print numbers
- Order of operation

Keywords
- Addition / Subtraction
- Multiplication / Division
- Order of operation
- Exponent / Power

```
Python 3.3.0 (v3.3.0:bd8afb90ebf2, Sep 29 2012, 10:57:17) [MSC v.1600 64 bit (AMD64)] on win32
Type "copyright", "credits" or "license()" for more information.
>>> print(7)
7
>>>
>>> print(2+4)
6
>>>
>>> print(10-3)
7
>>>
>>> print(4*3)
12
>>>
```

What you need to know before
- Simple mathematical calculations
- Order of operation

1.1 Let's write our first program

To find the value of any calculation in python we use the `print()` function. Python will evaluate mathematical statements and return the value of the calculations requested. The `print()` function is a built in function that print to the standard output device, which is the monitor in our case. We will discuss functions in more details in a later chapter. The `print()` function can also write to file or other streams.

Syntax:
```
print(<value>)
```

Where <value> can be a literal or a variable which in this case it will print the value stored at the memory location.

Examples:

Printing a number
```
>>> print(7)
7
>>>
```

Addition
```
>>> print(2+4)
6
>>>
```

Subtraction
```
>>> print(10-3)
7
>>>
```

Multiplication
```
>>> print(4*3)
12
>>>
```

Division
```
>>> print(12/3)
4.0
>>>
```

Exponent / Power
```
>>> print(5**2)
25
>>>
```

Floored Quotient

```
>>> print(7//2)
3
>>> print(1//2)
0
>>>
```

In mathematics if we divide 7 by 2 we get 3.5, if we want to get the floored quotient (round the answer down to the nearest whole number) in python we can use the floored quotient operator. Note that 1//2 will evaluate to 0 since in mathematics 1 divided by 2 is 0.5.

1.2   Order of operation

Python evaluates the correct order of operations therefore; it will give the correct answer to the calculation *3*4+2*.

```
>>> print(3*4+2)
14
>>>
```

> **Hint:** 3*4+2 and 3*(4+2) are two different questions Python knows and understand this and will interpret and print the correct result as seen below.

is quite different from

```
>>> print(3*(4+2))
18
>>>
```

The code below prints out the number of seconds in a week:

```
>>> print(7*24*60*60)
604800
>>>
```

PRACTICE EXERCISE 1

1. Write a program in python to print out the number of seconds in a 30 day month.

2. Write a program in python to print out the number of seconds in a year.

3. Use python as a calculator. The operations are just the same as what we are used to in mathematics.

4. A high speed train can travel at an average speed of 150 mph, how long will it take a train travelling at this speed to travel from London to Glasgow which is 414 miles away?
    a. Give your answer in minutes.

5. Using the help facility on python. Type help() to start the online facility, then keywords to view the keywords that are available in python. Get help on the "if" keyword.

6. Use the interpreter to execute the following:
    a. 49 / 7
    b. 8**2
    c. 20%3
    d. 17 // 3
    e. 7**3

7. Use python to evaluate the following:
    a. If you are going on holiday to France how much Euros would you get when you convert £500 at an exchange rate of £1 = €1.20.
    b. On return from your holiday you now have €320, how much GBP would you receive at an exchange rate of £1 = €1.32. Use python to calculate this.

8. The volume of a sphere is given by $V = \frac{4}{3}\pi r^3$, use python to find the volume of a sphere with a radius of 10 cm.

9. Insert brackets in the expression 36/9-2 to get:
    a. 2
    b. 5.12

Chapter 2: Values, Variables and Expressions

What we will learn:

- Definitions for values, variables and expressions
- Assigning values to variables
- Evaluate Expressions
- Store values in a statement

Keywords

- Values
- Expressions
- Statements
- Variables

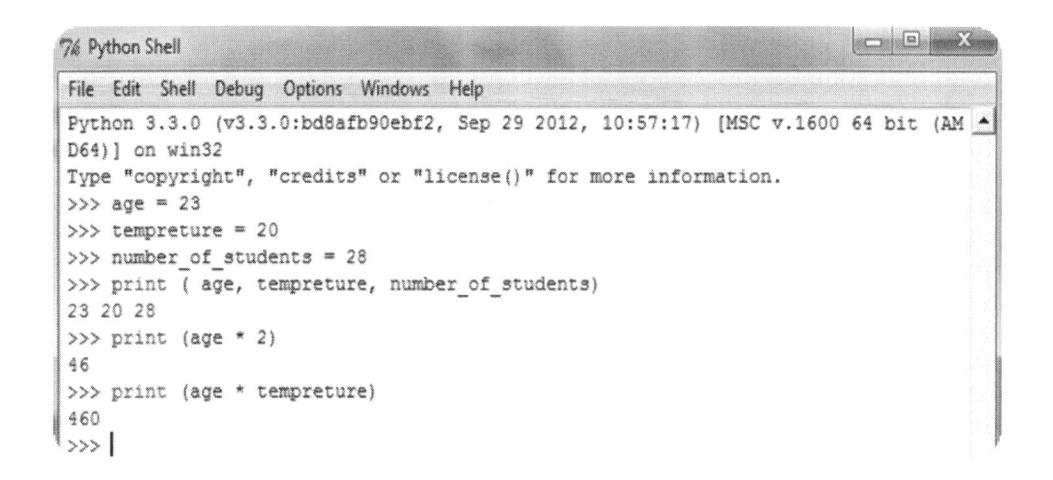

```
Python 3.3.0 (v3.3.0:bd8afb90ebf2, Sep 29 2012, 10:57:17) [MSC v.1600 64 bit (AMD64)] on win32
Type "copyright", "credits" or "license()" for more information.
>>> age = 23
>>> tempreture = 20
>>> number_of_students = 28
>>> print ( age, tempreture, number_of_students)
23 20 28
>>> print (age * 2)
46
>>> print (age * tempreture)
460
>>>
```

Subject Content	
3.1.1 Constants Variable and Data Types	• Constants • Variables

2.1   Definitions

Values are any literal that can be stored in a memory location. Values can be numeric, text consisting of characters, or special symbols. We often carry out operations on values. Examples of values are:

6
42
True
False
25

A **variable** is a named memory location. We assign values to variables. In python a variable must begin with a letter of the alphabet, it can also contain numbers and underscore but should not contain any space. We cannot use keywords for variable names these are reserved in memory for the program to use.

Words such as: *4value, my age, &sales and while* are all invalid and will generate a syntax error if you try to use them in python. This is because they meet the criteria of naming a variable but are reserved keywords. *Figure 3* shows a list of reserved keywords used in python:

Figure 3

```
>>> help('keywords')

Here is a list of the Python keywords.  Enter any keyword to get more help.

False               def                 if                  raise
None                del                 import              return
True                elif                in                  try
and                 else                is                  while
as                  except              lambda              with
assert              finally             nonlocal            yield
break               for                 not
class               from                or
continue            global              pass

>>>
```

We should also ensure that meaningful names are used so that one can remember what they represent. Examples of some meaningful names are:

age
height
name
length_of_room
item23
position23

These are all valid variable name, programmers normally use the underscore (_) character to separate long words as in *length_of_room* above. Another technique used is to join all

33

words together and begin each new word with a capital letter, for example `lengthOfRoom` is a legal variable.

An **expression** is a combination of operator and operations that evaluate to a value. Some examples of expressions are:

6

6+5

7*24

(3*23) + 20

a>b

An **assignment statement** is used to store the value of an expression in a variable. In python we assign an expression to a variable. For example

```
>>> age = 23
>>> temperature = 20
>>> number_of_students = 28
>>>
>>> minutes_in_a_year = 365*24*60
>>> marks = (3*15) + 12
>>>
```

Hint: The first line is read as age is assigned to 23. After making these assignment statements we can use these variables in our program.

Example: *print(age * 2)*

print(minutes_in_a_year * 60)

```
>>> print(age, temperature, number_of_students)
23 20 28
>>> print(minutes_in_a_year * 60)
31536000
>>> print(marks * 2)
114
>>>
```

In the example below we use a variable to store values of the length, width and the calculation of the area of a rectangle.

```
>>> length = 12
>>> width = 4
>>> area_of_rectangle = length *width
>>> print(area_of_rectangle)
48
>>>
```

In this example we use variables, expressions and statements to find out the total days alive (assuming all year have 365 days).

```
>>> age = 23
>>> number_of_days_alive = age *365
>>> print(number_of_days_alive)
8395
>>>
```

2.2 Multiple Assignments

Python allows us to do multiple assignments. Each statement on the right hand side is evaluated and the value stored in the corresponding variable on the left hand side.

```
>>> age, height = 23, 6
>>> print(age, height)
23 6
>>>
```

The values on the left are actually stored in a tuple (we will discuss this more when we meet list in chapter 4) then assigned to the variables on the right. This provides a neat solution for swapping values in python. For example

```
>>> age, height = 23, 6
>>> print(age, height)
23 6
>>> age, height = height, age
>>> print(age, height)
6 23
>>>
```

Notice that after the first assignment age has the value 23 and height has the value 6, after evaluating the statement

    `age, height = height, age`

The values are swapped and now age has the value of 6 and height has the value of 23. This is quite significant and in most other programming languages you will have to use a temporary variable to swap the values of two variables.

PRACTICE EXERCISE 2

1. Write a program that assigns the variables length and width to be 18 and 7 respectively. Use the variables to calculate the perimeter and area of the rectangle.

   > **Hint:** Perimeter = 2L + 2w   and
   >
   > Area = L x w

2. Write a python program that defines a variable called *days_in_school_each_year* and assign 192 to the variable. The program should then print out the total hours that you spend in school from year 7 to year 11, assuming that each day you spend 6 hours in school.

3. What value will be printed on the screen?
   ```
   marks = 25
   marks = marks + 10
   print(marks)
   ```

4. Given the code below, what value will be printed to the screen?
   ```
   time_spent = 34 # in minutes
   # after one minutes
   time_spent = time_spent +1
   print(time_spent)
   ```

   > **Note:** We use # to include comments in our code. Comments are ignored by the interpreter, they are meaningless to the interpreter, but give more information to us humans, this is particularly important for maintaining the code at a later date.

5. Which of the value below would be printed on the screen from the code snippet?
   a. 5040
   b. 210
   c. 720
   d. Error

   ```
   hours_in_a_week = hours_in_a_day * 7
   hours_in_a_month = hours_in_a_week * 30 # assuming we have 30 days in a month
   print (hours_in_a_month)
   ```
6. What is the value of score after running the following code?
   ```
   score = 24
   number_of_pieces = 2
   new_score = score *2
   ```

7. True or False: An expression can be assigned to a variable.
   What is the value of y after running the code?
   ```
   x, y = 23, 45
   y, x = x, y
   ```

8. Which of the following are not valid python variable name?

name	item34	4gs	country1
&item	_age	bestHeight	tHiSiSaVaRiAbLe

9. How do we use the help() function in python?

10. Which of the following statements will assign the value 365 to the variable days_in_a_year ?
    a. 365 = days_in_a_year
    b. there are 365 days in a year
    c. days in a year = 365
    d. Days_in_a_year = 365

37

Chapter 3: Data Types

What we will learn:

- Data type definition
- Use the type function to find out the data type of an object
- String operations

Keywords

- Float
- Integer
- String
- List
- Boolean

```
Python Shell
File  Edit  Shell  Debug  Options  Windows  Help
Python 3.3.0 (v3.3.0:bd8afb90ebf2, Sep 29 2012, 10:57:17) [MSC v.1600
D64)] on win32
Type "copyright", "credits" or "license()" for more information.
>>> value = 56.34
>>> type(value)
<class 'float'>
>>> month = "September"
>>> letter = month[1]
>>> print (letter)
e
```

Subject Content	Learning Outcomes
3.1.1 Constants Variable and Data Types	• Understand the different data types available to them • Be able to explain the purpose of data types

3.0 Data types in python

Data types tell the interpreter the range of value that can be stored and the kind of operations (addition, subtraction, comparison, concatenation, etc) that are possible on a given variable. *Table 2.1* shows some common data types used in python. They are also used in most other programming languages.

Table 2

Data Type	Values they store	Notation
Integers	Positive and negative whole numbers.	int
Floating Point Number	Stores any number that can be represented on the number line Decimal or fractional numbers	Float
List	Holds an array of data	[ ]
Boolean	True/ false values	
String	Sequence of character	Str

3.1 Integers

Integer is one of the three numeric types in python (int, float and complex). Integer is a built in data type which means there is no need to explicitly declare this, but python know how to deal with them naturally. We can find out the type of any object in python by using the `type ()`, function. The type function will return the data type of any given object. We will discuss the `class` in chapter 9.

```
>>> value = 35
>>> type(value)
<class 'int'>
>>>
```

We could declare value to be integer explicitly if we want, for example

```
>>> x = int(34)
>>> y = int(24.9)
>>> print(x, y, x-y)
34 24 10
>>>
```

We declare the variable value to be of type integer; notice that *24.9* will be truncated to an integer, and hence *24* will be stored in the variable y. In python integers have unlimited precision. *Table 3* summarizes the main operations that are defined for integers in python.

39

Table 3

Operation	Example	Explanation
Addition	x + y	Sum of x and y
Subtraction	x – y	Subtract y from x
Multiplication	x * y	Multiply x by y
Division	x / y	Divides x by y
Integer Division	x // y	Divides x by y and return the integer value only
Modulo	x % y	Remainder of x/y
Negate	-x	Negative value of x
Absolute value	abs(x)	Absolute value or magnitude of x
Cast	int(x)	x converted to an integer
Power	pow(x, y)	x raised to the power of y
Power	x **y	x raised to the power of y

3.2 Floating Point Number

Floating point numbers are similar to real numbers as encountered in mathematics. Visually the main difference is that a floating point number can have a decimal point. In python the floating point number is based on the data type called *double* in programming language C. The programming language implements data type based on the underlying machine and therefore the precision of float is machine dependent. We use the keyword *float* for floating point number in python.

```
>>> value = 56.34
>>> value
56.34
>>> type(value)
<class 'float'>
>>>
```

Similar to integers, there is no need to explicitly declare a variable to be of type float. Float has the same operations defined in *Table 3* above.

3.3 Strings

A String is a collection of characters. Strings are essential in all programming languages, and have a lot of operations defined over them. In python we use single or double quotation to denote literal strings.

Which quote to use?
Strings begin and end with single or double quotes. You must end with the type of quote that you begin with. This makes it possible to include quotation within a text. For example:

```
>>> message = "Hello Ben I'm happy to learn about string today"
>>> print(message)
Hello Ben I'm happy to learn about string today
>>>
```

Python also allows users to use single quote in a text to allow the use the use of quotations. Example:

```
>>> message = 'Martin Luther famous speech "I have a dream" is very inspirational'
>>> print(message)
Martin Luther famous speech "I have a dream" is very inspirational
>>>
```

> **Hint:** Begin and end the quote with the same quotation marks

3.3.1 Assigning String to a Variable

The following code assigns the string September to the variable month:

```
>>> month = "September"
>>> month
'September'
>>>
```

It is possible to use square brackets and index number to access individual characters in a string.

```
>>> month = "September"
>>> print(month)
September
>>> letter = month[1]
>>> print(letter)
e
>>>
```

Above we assign *letter* to `month[1]`, and the letter `e` is printed. This may be surprising as 'e' is the second character in the word *'September'*, it turns out that the first position in a string is position 0, therefore the word September is stored in this manner in python.

Position →	0	1	2	3	4	5	6	7	8
Content	S	e	p	t	e	m	b	e	r

A loop can be used to go through the string month, we will discuss the "for loop" in details in chapter 5 when we discuss Control Structures.

`month = "September"` will make this assignment

```
>>> month
'September'
>>> i=0
>>> for letter in month:
        print(month[i])
        i=i+1

S
e
p
t
e
m
b
e
r
>>>
```

The emphasis here is on the values of i, notice that first time `i` is assigned to 0 and therefore the first print statement will execute `month[0]`.

> **Hint:** Whenever you see negative index python start from the end of the list with the last character being -1, therefore.
>
> `print month[-3]`

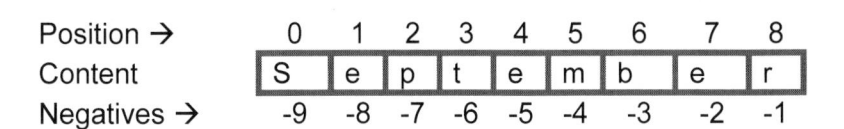

Position →	0	1	2	3	4	5	6	7	8
Content	S	e	p	t	e	m	b	e	r
Negatives →	-9	-8	-7	-6	-5	-4	-3	-2	-1

What will `month[-5]` print?

> **Hint:** Both `month[10]` and `month[-10]` will give an "out of range error".
>
> IndexError: string index out of range

42

```
>>> month = "September"
>>> month[10]
Traceback (most recent call last):
  File "<pyshell#69>", line 1, in <module>
    month[10]
IndexError: string index out of range
>>> month[-10]
Traceback (most recent call last):
  File "<pyshell#70>", line 1, in <module>
    month[-10]
IndexError: string index out of range
>>>
```

Index error is a common programming error and should be avoided.

3.4 Other string operations

3.4.1 Sub-sequence

In python we can select a sub-sequence of a string by using a colon in the square brackets to denote the start and end the position that is required. Python will print the first position and stop just before the end position. If we leave the start position out then python will start from the beginning of the string to the end position; in a similar manner if we leave the end position out then python select up to the last character in the string.

Syntax

    <string>[<start position>:<end position>]

Example

```
>>> month = "September"
>>> month[3:6]
'tem'
>>> month[:6]
'Septem'
>>> month[6:]
'ber'
>>>
```

3.4.2   Finding string within string

The **find()** method returns an integer that represents the starting position of where a sub-string occurs in a string, if the sub-string is not contained in the string then -1 is returned.

syntax
```
<string>.find(<substring>)
```

Example:
```
>>> hoyle='It is the true nature of mankind to learn from his mistakes'
>>> hoyle.find('nature of mankind')
15
>>> hoyle.find('for every actions')
-1
>>>
```

3.4.3   Finding the length of a string

The `len()` method returns the number of characters in a string; this include spaces and special characters. `Len()` is an operator that can be used on any collection of objects such as List that we will discuss in chapter 6.

syntax
```
len(<string>)
```

Example:
```
>>> month='September'
>>> len(month)
9
>>>
```

3.5   Upper case character

The **upper()** method returns a copy of the string with all letters in uppercase.

syntax
```
<string>.upper()
```

Example:
```
>>> month='September'
>>> month.upper()
'SEPTEMBER'
>>>
```

3.5.1 Lower case character

The **lower()** method returns a copy of the string with all letters in lowercase.

syntax
```
<string>.lower()
```

Example:

```
>>> month='Septemebr'
>>> month.lower()
'septemebr'
>>>
```

3.5.2 Concatenate String (+)

Concatenation refers to joining two or more strings together. We use the "*+ operator*" to do this in python. Concatenation cannot be used for string and numeric data type together.

syntax
```
<string> + <string>
```

Example:
```
>>> greeting = 'hello '
>>> name = 'Benjamin'
>>> greeting + name
'hello Benjamin'
>>>
```

```
>>> 'hello' + 15

Traceback (most recent call last):
  File "<pyshell#14>", line 1, in <module>
    'hello' + 15
TypeError: cannot concatenate 'str' and 'int' objects
>>>
```

The error above is a *type error*, this happen whenever you try to apply an operation that is not defined over the data type, in this case whenever you try to concatenate string and integers.

Hint: You cannot add a numeric value to a string

Multiplication is defined for string and integers.
```
>>> 'hello ' *3
'hello hello hello '
>>>
```

3.6 Testing for membership using the in operator

The in operator is used to test for membership within a given sequence. The in operator is not specific to string but can be used with any collection of objects. The in operator will return TRUE, if the element is found and FALSE otherwise.

The following code test to see if 'p' appears in the word September.

```
>>> month = "September"
>>> 'p' in month
True
>>> 'v' in month
False
>>>
```

From the code snippet above seen that `'p'` appears in `September`, `True` is returned and `False` is returned when we test if `'v'` appears in the word.

3.7 Converting Data type

int()

To convert from one data type to another the built functions are used. To convert to an integer, we use the `int()` function.

syntax
    `int(<value>)`

Where <value> is the value to be converted to an integer; python will convert this value if it can, otherwise it will give an error message.

Example:

```
>>> value= '45'
>>> type(value)
<class 'str'>
>>> type( int(value))
<class 'int'>
>>>
```

Note that we assign value to the string '45', this is confirmed by using the `type()` function to check. On the forth line we check the type of `int(value)`. This statement `int(value)`, converted the string to an integer and hence `int` will print as the type. It is not possible to convert all values to string as we can see from the example below.

46

```
>>> type( int('Hello'))
Traceback (most recent call last):
  File "<pyshell#134>", line 1, in <module>
    type( int('Hello'))
ValueError: invalid literal for int() with base 10: 'Hello'
>>>
```

We can convert floating point number to integer.

```
>>> value = 45.9483738
>>> type(value)
<class 'float'>
>>> type( int(value))
<class 'int'>
>>> int(value)
45
>>>
```

Note that `int()` will convert floating point number but in the conversion python does truncation, in that the number is not rounded up or down, the whole number is simply taken and the rest of the number is ignored.

float()

float() will convert a given value to a floating point number.

syntax
> *float(<value>)*

Where <value> is the value to be converted to a floating point number; python will convert this value if it can, otherwise it will give an error message.

Example:

```
>>> float(32)
32.0
>>>
```

str()
str() will convert a given value to a string.

syntax
> *str(<value>)* where <value> is the value to be converted to a string.

Example:

```
>>> str(45)
'45'
>>>
```

Note that the '45' is now a string.

3.8 Taking input from the user

input()

We use the input() function to prompt the user for data. We can then assign this data to a variable. The default expected value is a string and therefore the converters discussed in *section 3.3* above would have to be used to change the data to the required type if this is possible.

syntax
```
input("<prompt>" )
```

Where <prompt> is the message to be printed on the screen; python will take input from the standard input (keyboard).

Example:
```
>>> name = input("What is your name? ")
What is your name? Benjamin
>>> print("Hello " + name)
Hello Benjamin
>>>
```

In the following example the program ask the user to enter two numbers then print the sum to the screen, note that this will require type conversion.

```
>>> number1 = int( input("Please enter the first number: "))
Please enter the first number: 45
>>> number2 = int( input("Please enter the second number: "))
Please enter the second number: 12
>>> print("The sum is ", number1+number2)
The sum is  57
>>>
```

Practice Exercise 3

1. Write a python program that stores your favourite quotation in a variable called quote.

2. Define a variable called name that assigns your name to it.

3. Write a python program that ask the user for three numbers and print their sum.

4. Write a python program that ask the user for their name and age and print this back to the screen with a warm message.

5. What is the data type of x in the code snippet below?
```
>>> x = 34.67
>>>
```

6. What letter will be printed on the screen after running the following code?
```
>>> title = "Python for key stage 4"
>>> letter = title[3]
>>> print(letter)
```

7. What letter will be printed on the screen after running the code?
```
>>> title = "Python for key stage 4"
>>> letter = title[-5]
>>> print(letter)
```

8. Use the slice operation / sub-sequence to print "key" from the variable title.
    a. Title = "GCSE Python"

9. Use the variable below and the concatenation operation to print the greetings below.
    b. Name = "Benjamin"
Greetings to print: "Hello Benjamin, Python is fun"

10. What will the following code produce?

```
title= "GCSE Python"
for letter in title:
   print(letter)
```

49

Chapter 4 : Functions

What we will learn:
- Definition of a function
- Syntax of functions
- Return values from a function

Keywords
- Function
- Return

```
Python Shell
File Edit Shell Debug Options Windows Help
Python 3.3.0 (v3.3.0:bd8afb90ebf2, Sep 29 2012, 10:57:17) [MSC v.1600
D64)] on win32
Type "copyright", "credits" or "license()" for more information.
>>> def sum(a,b):
        return a + b

>>> sum (12 , 19)
31
>>> sum ("Hello", " Bobby")
'Hello Bobby'
```

Subject Content	Learning Outcomes
3.1.4 Procedures and Functions • What procedures and functions are • When to use procedures and functions • Writing your own procedures and functions. • Built in functions • Parameters • Return values	• Understand what procedures and functions are in programming terms. • Know when the use of a procedure or function would make sense and would simplify the coded solution. • Know how to write and use their own simple procedures and functions. • Know about and be able to describe common built in functions in their chosen language(s). • Use common built in functions in their chosen language(s) when coding solutions to problems. • Understand what a parameter is when working with procedures and functions. • Know how to use parameters when creating efficient solutions to problems. • Understand the concepts of parameters and return values when working with procedures and functions

4.1 Definition

Functions are a block of codes that perform a specific task. It allows us to re-use it and carry out a set of computation more than once. Functions take in an input and can return an output. They can also take in multiple inputs or no input; have multiple outputs or no outputs at all. Python provides a lot of useful functions for us such as `print()`, `type()`, `abs()`, these functions are called built-in because they are supplied as part of the language. We can declare and define our own function to do what we want them to do. Functions that are defined by a user are called user defined function. This chapter will focus on user defined functions.

4.1.1 Why do we use functions?

- Using functions make our program code more readable. When we define a function we are actually naming certain set of instruction that are performing a specific task and therefore making our program code easier to read.

- Functions can reduce our program code significantly by putting repetitive code into a function.
- Change or adjustments can be made in one place.

- Functions facilitate modular design. We can break down a large problem into manageable chunks, work on these chunks in functions then put the entire working piece together for a working solution.

- Function can be placed into modules so that they can be reused.

4.1.2 Function Syntax

syntax
```
def <name>(<ParameterList>):
    <block>
    return <expression>, <expression>
```

Where `<name>` follows the same conventions as a variable

`<ParameterList>` represents the inputs to the function separated by comma. The return statement is used to specify the output. By default all functions return a value. If one is not specified using the return keyword then `None` is automatically returned.
`return <expression>, <expression>, ...`

> **Hint:** Functions must begin with a letter of the alphabet and cannot contain space

```
>>> def sum(a, b):
        return a+b
>>> sum(12, 10)
22
>>>
```

Whenever we express what the function should do we call this **defining a function**. The function in the example is defining the function sum. The 'a' and 'b' are referred to as **parameters** and are only valid variables within the definition of the function; the range of the area that the variable is valid is called the **scope of the variable**. Note that 'a' and 'b' are place holders and is only valid within the definition.

Whenever we use a function this is referred to as **calling a function**. In the example above `sum(12, 10)` is a call to the function with arguments 12 and 10.

4.1.3   Returning values

We can define functions that just do something without explicitly returning a value, for example the following function will take a name and say hello twice.

```
>>> def hello_twice(name):
        print("Hello "+name)
        print("Hello "+name)


>>> print(hello_twice("Ahmed"))
Hello Ahmed
Hello Ahmed
None
>>>
```

Notice that after calling the function `None` is printed as the returned value. It turns out that because we did not use the return keyword in the function definition, then `None` is returned automatically.

4.2   Parameters and Arguments

Some books will use parameter and arguments interchangeably; however, there is a difference. It turns out that parameters are the place holders that are used in defining the function, whereas the arguments are the actual values that are supplied during the function call. Parameters are specific to function definition, in fact the parameters are data type (defines acceptable range and operations) whereas an argument is an instance of the parameter and is used in the function call. Notice that the argument can change with each function call, and is normally executed at run-time.

Python also uses a technique called operator overloading, where operators such as the + can be defined to perform different operation based on the operands that surrounds it. Since + is defined for strings also (namely concatenation) then the following will result in sum concatenating the strings that it receives.

```
>>> sum('Hello', ' Bobby')
'Hello Bobby'
```

This is a very powerful concept in object oriented programming and python being an object oriented language utilises these features.

> **Hint:**
> In the definition sum(a,b), a and b are the parameters while in the call sum(4,5), 4 and 5 are the arguments

4.3 Saving your program code

Python can operate in two modes, namely the interactive mode and the script mode. You know that you are in script mode if you have the three chevrons (>>>), and the blinking cursor. In this mode you type and at the end of the statement python interprets and produces a result. All of the examples so far have been in interactive mode. You can create a python file, type all your program code here and then interpret this file. This allows us to make changes and rerun the script. The instructions below will demonstrate how to create a script file.

From the python interpreter you can `select file` → `new window` to start a new window that you can type your program code into.

Save this file with a suitable file name and `.py` as the file extension, this will tell the interpreter that this file is a python file. Once you are finish typing your program code you can execute your program by selecting `run` → `run module`, your output will be displayed in the python interpreter.

Example: Creating a new script file

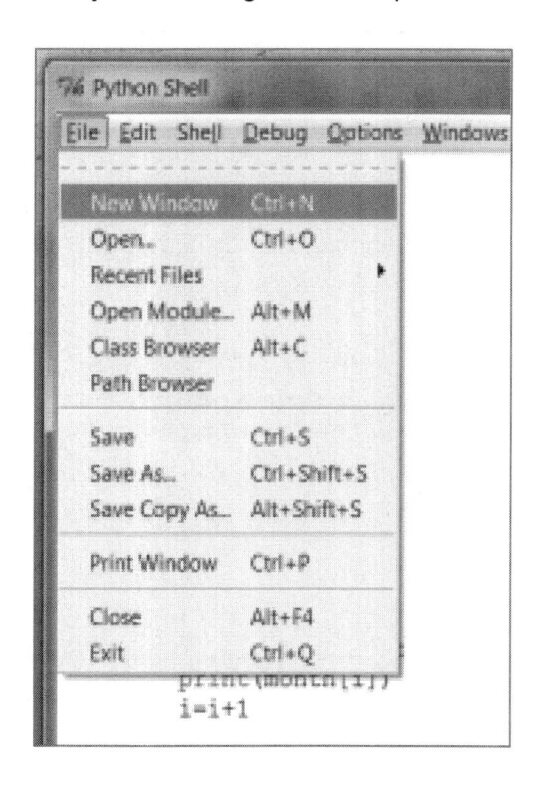

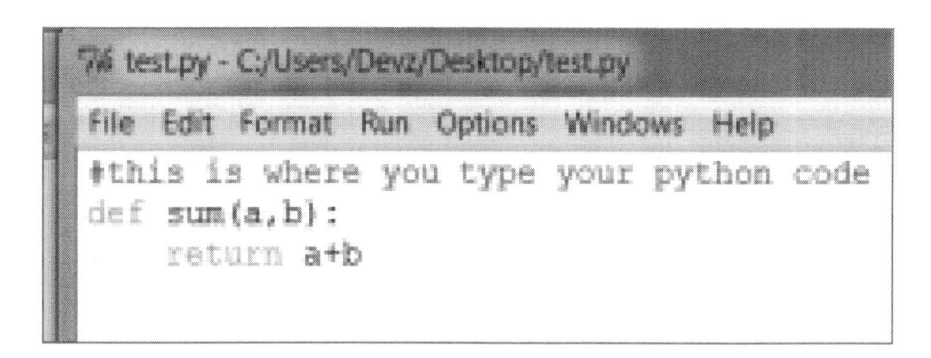

```
#this is where you type your python code
def sum(a,b):
    return a+b
```

After typing your script you can run and make changes to this.

Hint: If we need to add other numbers we simply call the sum function. Python is very dynamic and can reuse the function with strings. For example calling the sum function with two strings will return both strings concatenated seen that + is defined for strings.

4.4 Program Flow

A program is executed from top to bottom; line by line unless the flow is diverted by some control structure (we will examine control structure in chapter 6). It turns out that functions do not affect the program flow. When a function is called then execution jumps to the definition of the program and replace the argument(s) with the parameter(s) (recall that the parameters are place holder whereas arguments are the actual values that are sent to the program), the body of the program is executed then execution continue after the line that calls the function.

This process seems pretty straight forward, but when you imagine that a function can call another function who in turn can call other functions then keeping track of where you are can be quite complex. Further in python you can send a function as an argument to another function. It turns out that python has a very efficient method of handling this situation. Here are two simple examples that should demonstrate this point, but you can imagine that this could be more complex calculations.

Image that we have a function called larger that returns the larger of two given numbers, then

```
>>> x = 12
>>> y = 7
>>> z = 79
>>> print(larger(larger(x,y),z))
79
>>>
```

This will print the largest of the three numbers. In the example above you can see that the inner `larger(x,y)` was an argument to the outer larger function. The outer larger function would execute an instance of the larger function returning the value 12, seen that 12 is larger than 7, then the outer larger would evaluate `larger(12,79)` and finally return 79 to the print function.

PRACTICE EXERCISE 4

1. Define a function called double, that takes a number and return the number doubled.

2. Define a function called perimeter_of_rectangle that takes two numbers to represent the length and width of a rectangle and return the perimeter of the rectangle. (Remember that perimeter is twice the length added to twice the width).

3. Define a function called area_of_circle that takes one number as input to represent the radius, and return the area of the circle. (Remember that area of a circle is 22/7 * r^2).

4. Define a function called hello_three_times that takes an argument called name, and print hello name, three times on the screen.

5. Write a program that requests from the user their name. The program should then use a function called head_name(), that print the first character from the given name.

6. Write a program that asks the user for his name. The program should then use a function called tail_name(), that return the tail of the person's name where the tail of the name is the person's name without the first character.
HINT: len(<string>) will return the length of a string.

7. Give three advantages of using functions in a program.

8. What is the difference between parameter and arguments?

9. Define a function called power_value(), that takes two integers and return the first raised to the power of the second.

10. If we had a function called absolute_value(), that takes a number and return the positive value of the given number. What value will be returned for the following print statements?
    ```
    print(absolute_value(-5))
    print(absolute_value(0))
    print(-absolute_value(-5))
    ```

CHAPTER 5 : CONTROL STRUCTURES

What we will learn:
- Selection Structures
- Loops

Keywords
- For loop
- While loops
- If Selection
- If/else Structures

```
File  Edit  Shell  Debug  Options  Windows  Help
Python 3.3.0 (v3.3.0:bd8afb90ebf2, Sep 29 2012, 10:57:
[MSC v.1600 64 bit (AMD64)] on win32
Type "copyright", "credits" or "license()" for more in
mation.
>>> if 5>2:
        print ("5 is larger")


5 is larger
>>> month = "September"
>>> if len(month)>10:
        print (month + "has more than 10 characters")
else:
        print (month + "has less than 10 characters")
```

Subject Content	Learning Outcomes
3.1.3 Program Flow Control • Sequencing • Selection • iteration	• Understand the need for structure when designing coded solutions to problems. • Understand and be able to describe the basic building blocks of coded solutions (ie sequencing, selection and iteration) • Know when to use different flow control blocks (ie sequencing, selection and iteration) to solve problems

Control structures are used to affect the natural program flow. In this section we will discuss a number of control structures that are available in python.

5.1 Selection or Conditional Statements

The first type of control structure that we will evaluate is statements. Selection statements execute a particular block of code based on the result from some test / condition. The two selection statements that we will be exploring are IF and IF ELSE statements.

5.1.1 IF Statement

When using the IF statement we test to see if one condition is true or false. This is called a conditional test. The IF statement execute a block of statement based on the result from a conditional test. The If statement will only execute if the condition is true. Below is the syntax for an IF statement:

Syntax:
```
if <condition>:
    <block>
```

> **Hint:** The block is only executed whenever the condition is true.

Example:

```
>>> if 5>2:
        print("5 is larger")

5 is larger
>>>
```

> **Hint:** The statement '5 is larger' is printed to the screen since 5 is indeed greater than 2.

5.1.2   IF ELSE Statement

The IF ELSE statement is an extension to the IF statement, it will execute a block when a condition is true and an alternate block if the condition is false.

syntax
```
if <condition>:
    <TrueBlock>
else:
    <FalseBlock>
```

Where `<TrueBlock>` is executed if the condition is true and `<FalseBlock>` is executed when the condition is false.

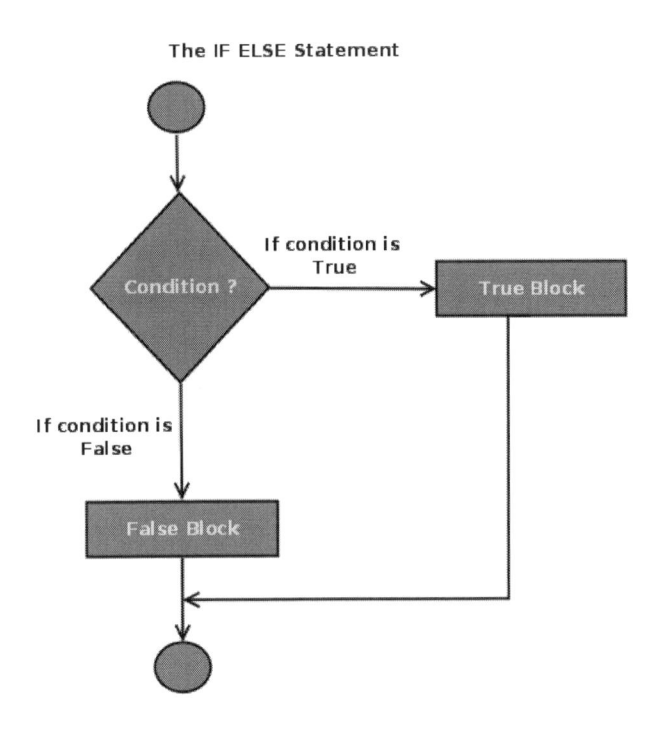

The IF ELSE Statement

Example:
```
>>> month = 'September'
>>> if len(month)>10:
        print(month + ' has more than ten characters ')
else:
        print(month + ' has less than ten characters ')

September has less than ten characters
>>>
```

Hint: Note that *len(month)* will evaluate to 9 and therefore the condition will be false, and hence printing the else clause.

5.2 Loops

Loops allow us to execute a block of code a number of times. Each time the set of instruction is executed is called **iteration.** Python offers two looping statements namely; the for loop and the while loop.

5.2.1 For Loop

For loop iterate over the items in a sequence, which can be a string or a list (we will discuss list in chapter 6), each time assigning the values in this sequence to a given variable. Note that the terminating condition is that we are at the end of the list.

syntax
```
for <variable> in <sequence>:
    <block>
```

Where `<variable>` is a variable that is assigned to each value in the sequence.
and `<sequence>` is a string or a list.
`<block>` is executed each time through the loop

Example:
```
>>> month = 'September'
>>> for letter in month:
        print(letter)

S
e
p
t
e
m
b
e
r
>>>
```

Example:

If we want to print the month of September, we would assign a variable to iterate the loop and print the values in the list.

The first time it iterates through the loop `'S'` is assigned to the variable `letter`, and hence the `print()` function will print `'S'`.

The second time through the loop `'e'` is assigned to the variable `letter` and will print `e`.

The third time through the loop `'p'` is assigned to the variable `letter` and will print `p`.

The fourth time through the loop `'t'` is assigned to the variable `letter` and will print `t`.

This continues to the end of the loop. This is determined by the length of the word.

Notice that we go through the body of the for loop (`print letter`) nine times and each time we print the letters in the assigned string.

5.2.2 The range function

The built in range function is very useful with the for loop and is used to iterate over a sequence of numbers.

syntax

```
range(<start>, <stop>,<step>)
```

Where `<start>` is optional and if it is not present will default to start at zero (0).
`<stop>` is not optional and is never included in the generated sequence.
`<step>` can be used to change the default increment from one (1) to another number

Example:

```
>>> print(range(10))
range(0, 10)
>>>
>>> #Now we use range() in a for loop
>>> for i in range(10):
        print(i)


0
1
2
3
4
5
6
7
8
9
>>>
```

Notice that `print(range(10))` will generate a virtual tuple from 0-10; and the for loop will iterate through this list 10 times.

5.3.1 While Loop

While loops are used in situations in which the number of iterations is unknown. It will execute a block as long as a given condition is true.

syntax
```
while <condition>:
    <block>
```

While loops evaluates whether an expression or condition is true or false. The block is evaluated until the condition becomes false.

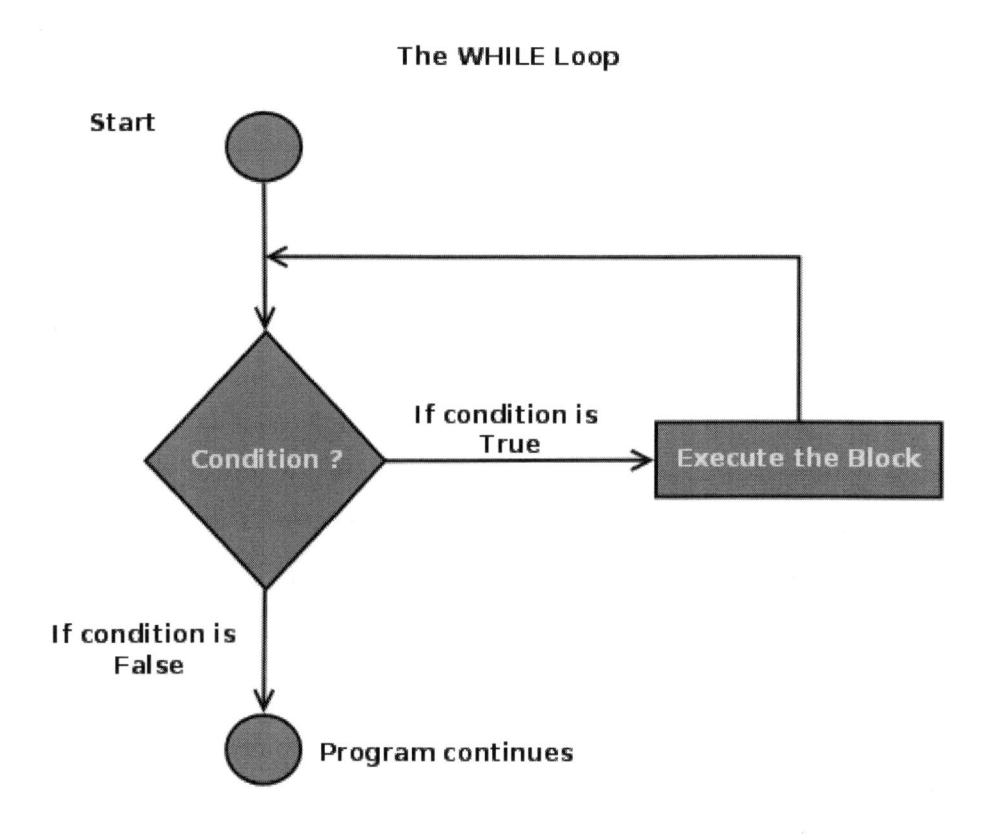

The WHILE Loop

[Flowchart: Start → Condition? → If True: Execute the Block (loops back to Condition); If False: Program continues]

> **Important:** There must be statements within the while loop that will allow the condition to become false or else we could be in a situation where a loop execute forever.

62

Example:

```
>>> number = 1
>>> while number < 11:
        print(number * number) #Square the number
        number = number + 1

1
4
9
16
25
36
49
64
81
100
>>>
```

Here we use the while loop to print the square numbers from 1 to 100. Notice that the statement `number = number +1`, will ensure that the condition will become false at some stage.

The `#square the number` is a comment. Comments are ignored by the interpreter; we use them to give more explanation to someone reading our program code.

5.3.2 Break

Break allow us to exit the while loop even when the condition is true. Break should be used with caution and should only be used if there is no alternative.

Typical use
```
while <condition>:
    <code>
    If <BreakTest>:
        Break
    <code>
<code after while loop>
```

Here during the while loop, if the break test is met then execution will jump out of the while loop and code after the while loop will be executed.

Example:

```
z=[2,5,7,1,90]

def find_seven(p):
    i=0
    while i!=len(p):
        if p[i]==7:
            print("Breaking out of Loop")
            print("Found at position ", i)
            break
        i=i+1
    print("After the while")

find_seven(z)
```

When we run the code above calling `find_seven(z)`, the following output will be produced.

```
>>> ================================ RESTART ================================
>>>
Breaking out of Loop
Found at position  2
After the while
>>>
```

Notice that 7 is at position 2 in the list and once we find 7 we exit the while loop, even though the while condition (`i!=len(p)`) was still true seen that i is 2 and `len(p)` is 5.

Practise Exercise 5

1. Write a python program that ask the user to enter two numbers, It will use the IF/ELSE statement to print the larger of the two.

2. Write a python program that asks the user to enter a score, it should print the following message, base on the score of the user:
    a. 50 and above - → "Pass"
    b. 0-49   → "Fail"

3. Develop the program in b) above by using a nested IF statement (IF within IF), to give the following additional information:
    a. 50 and above   → "Pass"
        i. 80+   →"Well Done"

    b. 0 – 49   → "Fail"
        i. <20   → "You need to try harder"
4. Write a python program that ask the user for a score and print a grade based on the following:

    | 80-100 | A |
    | 60 – 79 | B |
    | 40 – 59 | C |
    | 30 – 39 | D |
    | < 30 | U |

5. Suppose we calculate the vowel worth of a word based on the following rubric:

    | a | 5 points |
    | e | 4 points |
    | i | 3 points |
    | o | 2 points |
    | u | 1 points |

    Write a python program that ask the user for a word, then calculate and print the vowel worth of the word entered.

6. Define a function called *larger()*, that takes two integers and return the larger of the two.

7. Define a function called *long_name()* that take a name is input and return a Boolean value (True or False) based on the number of characters in the name. Assume a name is long if it contains more than 14 characters.

8. Define a function called *largest()* that takes three numbers and return the largest of the three. HINT: You can write the function from scratch of use the *larger()* function that was written before.

9. Write a function called *print_upto()* that takes a number as input and print all the whole numbers from 1 up to and including the given number.

10. Write a function called ***print_even_upto()*** that takes a number as input and print all the **even** numbers from 1 up to and including the given number.

11. Write a function called ***magic_number()*** that has a variable assigned to the value 7, The user should be prompted to guess the magic number. The program should give the user feedback on the guess.
    i. If the guess is greater than 7, "Too high"
    ii. If the guess is less than 7, "Too low"
    iii. If the guess is correct it should print "Well Done"

12. Modify the program above to give the user only 5 guesses, If more that 5 guesses then the user should get the following message "you have gotten your maximum chances" this information should be provided to the user.

13. The factorial of a number is the product of all the integers below it. For example the factorial of 4 is 4*3*2*1 = 24.
    a. Write a function called ***factorial()*** that returns the factorial of the given number.
    b. ***factorial(4)*** → 24

CHAPTER 6 : LIST

What we will learn:
- List Definition
- Syntax for creating list
- Selecting elements of a list
- Selecting subsequence of a list

Keywords
- List
- Sub-list
- Elements
- Index
- Position

```
Python 3.3.0 (v3.3.0:bd8afb90ebf2, Sep 29 2012, 10:57:17) [MSC v.1600 64 bit (AMD64)] on win32
Type "copyright", "credits" or "license()" for more information.
>>> days = ["Sunday", "Monday", "Tuesday", "Wednesday", "Thursday", "Friday", "Saturday"]
>>> days
['Sunday', 'Monday', 'Tuesday', 'Wednesday', 'Thursday', 'Friday', 'Saturday']
>>> days [0]
'Sunday'
>>> days[-2]
'Friday'
>>> days[5:]
['Friday', 'Saturday']
>>> days [2:5]
['Tuesday', 'Wednesday', 'Thursday']
```

Subject Content	Learning Outcomes
3.1.2 Structures • How data types can be combined to make data structures • How data structures can make coding a solution to a problem simpler	• Be able to explain what a data structure is. • Be able to produce their own data structure that go beyond the built in structure of the language they are using. • Understand and be able to explain why data structures can make coding a solution simpler.

6.1 Definition

The list is the most versatile data structure python uses. It is a mutable collection of data items, which can be of the same or different data types. When a data collection is mutable it means we can change individual items in the collection. The items are written between square brackets and are separated by comma; they can be assigned to a variable.

syntax
```
<variable> = [<list_item>, <list_item>, ...]
```

Where `<list_item>` can be empty, or any data type.

Example:
```
>>> days = ["Sunday", "Monday", "Tuesday", "Wednesday", "Thursday", "Friday", "Saturday"]
>>> days
['Sunday', 'Monday', 'Tuesday', 'Wednesday', 'Thursday', 'Friday', 'Saturday']
>>>
```

6.1.1 Selecting individual elements

Because list is a compound data type we can select individual elements by indexing these.
```
>>> days[0]
'Sunday'
>>>
```

Using negative index
Negative index will return the value at the position from the end of the list.
```
>>> days[-2]
'Friday'
>>>
```

6.2 List operations

Concatenation
We can concatenate list by using the concatenation operation (+).

```
>>> x = [1, 2, 3]
>>> y = [6, 7, 8]
>>> z = x+y    #Concatenation Operation
>>> print(z)
[1, 2, 3, 6, 7, 8]
>>>
```

Notice that z now store the items of x and y.

Multiplication
Multiplication operation has a similar effect on list as on strings.

```
>>> x = [1, 2, 3]
>>> print(x*3)
[1, 2, 3, 1, 2, 3, 1, 2, 3]
>>>
>>> print(x*4)
[1, 2, 3, 1, 2, 3, 1, 2, 3, 1, 2, 3]
>>>
```

Notice that multiplying by three produces three of the list.

6.3.1 Selecting a sub-sequence in the list – Slicing

We can select a sub-sequence in a list by using the slice operation. The slice operation (:), is used to specify the starting point and the end point to return a section of a list.

```
>>> days
['Sunday', 'Monday', 'Tuesday', 'Wednesday', 'Thursday', 'Friday', 'Saturday']
>>> days[2:5]
['Tuesday', 'Wednesday', 'Thursday']
>>> days[:4]
['Sunday', 'Monday', 'Tuesday', 'Wednesday']
>>> days[5:]
['Friday', 'Saturday']
>>>
```

Sub-selection is also called slicing the list. It is important to note that sub-selection will return a virtual copy of the list and does not mutate the original list, from the example above days is unaffected hence printing the value of days will give the entire list.

```
>>> days
['Sunday', 'Monday', 'Tuesday', 'Wednesday', 'Thursday', 'Friday', 'Saturday']
>>>
```

> **Important:** The first number in the slice operation *[<start> : <end>]* is the starting point and the last number is the ending point. If these are left blank then python assumes that the start position is the beginning of the list and the end position is the end of the list.

6.4   Editing a list

Because lists are mutable unlike strings it is possible to change the values in a list.

```
>>> a=[1,3,5]
>>> a
[1, 3, 5]
>>> a[1] = 25 # Change the value at position 1
>>> a #This is the updated a
[1, 25, 5]
>>>
```

Note that we can assign new elements to a list by referring to its position and assigning a new value.

6.5   List of List

Python allows us to have list of list

```
>>> olympic_host = [["London",2012], ["Beijing",2008], ["Athens",2004]]
>>> olympic_host
[['London', 2012], ['Beijing', 2008], ['Athens', 2004]]
>>> olympic_host[1] #print the first element in the list
['Beijing', 2008]
>>> olympic_host[1][0] #element in pos 0 in the list at pos 1
'Beijing'
>>>
```

We make a few observations from the script above.
- It is possible to have different data types in the same list, above we used string and an integer to represent a year.
- We can have list of list `Olympic_host` is a list containing three elements where each element is itself a list containing the Olympic host city and year.
- We can access the individual element in each list by sub-indexing the position in the example above `Olympic_host[1][0]`

6.6 List methods

There are various methods defined on list, below we will examine some of these methods.

append()
Append will add an element to the end of the list. Append mutate (change) the list instead of creating a new list, the result of invoking append on a list is that the calling list will have the new element added to the end.

syntax
```
<list>.append(<element>)
```

Where `<list>` is the list to be appended.
and `<element>` is the element to be appended to the list

Example:
```
>>> x=[3,6,2,15,20]
>>> print(x)
[3, 6, 2, 15, 20]
>>> x.append(45)
>>> print(x)
[3, 6, 2, 15, 20, 45]
>>>
```

Notice that after a call to append with argument 45, the list x now have 45 appended to the end.

insert()
Insert is used to insert an element at a given index. Insert mutate the existing list with the new element inserted.

syntax
```
<list>.insert(<position>, <element>)
```

Where `<list>` is the list to that the element should be inserted into.
   `<position>` is the position in the list that the element will be inserted, recall that the first position is position zero (0)
   `<element>` is the element to be inserted into the list

Example:

```
>>> print(x)
[3, 6, 2, 15, 20, 45]
>>> x.insert(3,35)
>>> print(x)
[3, 6, 2, 35, 15, 20, 45]
>>>
```

Notice that after the insert function is invoked on the list x, 35 is now inserted in position 3.

sort()

Sort function will sort the list.

syntax

<list>.sort()

Where *<list>* is the list to be sorted.

Example:

```
>>> y=[35, 30, 23, 38, 10, 15, 2]
>>> print(y)
[35, 30, 23, 38, 10, 15, 2]
>>> y.sort()
>>> print(y)
[2, 10, 15, 23, 30, 35, 38]
>>>
```

count()

Count will return the number of occurrence of an element in a list.

syntax

<list>.count(<element>)

Where *<list>* is the list that count is invoked on
<element> is the element that you search for the occurrence of.

Example:

```
>>> y
[2, 10, 15, 23, 30, 35, 38, 2]
>>> y
[2, 10, 15, 23, 30, 35, 38, 2]
>>> y.count(2)
2
>>> y.count(15)
1
>>> y.count(45)
0
```

Notice that there are two occurrences of 2, and only one of occurrence of 15 there are no 45 in the list and hence *y.count(45)* will return 0.

72

extend()
Extend mutate a list and have the effect of adding a second list to the first list. Note that the second list will still exist, in its original state.

syntax
```
<list1>.extend(<list2>)
```

Where `<list1>` is the list to be mutated.
  `<list2>` is the list that will be added to list 1.

Example:
```
>>> x=[1,2,3,4]
>>> y=[5,6,7]
>>> x
[1, 2, 3, 4]
>>> y
[5, 6, 7]
>>> x.extend(y)
>>> x
[1, 2, 3, 4, 5, 6, 7]
>>> y
[5, 6, 7]
```

After `x.extend(y)` is called x now contains the elements of both x and y, however y is unchanged and still exist.

pop()
The pop method will remove and return an element from the list. By default *pop()* invoked on a list will remove and return the last element in a list. You can optionally send the index on an element to be removed from the list and *pop()* will return that element.

syntax
```
<list>.pop()
    OR
<list>.pop([<index>])
```

Where `<list>` is the list with the elements
  `<index>` is the optional position of the element to be removed from the list

Example:
```
>>> x
[8, 5, 12, 9, 20]
>>> x.pop()   #Now we invoke pop() on list x
20
>>> x # print the list x
[8, 5, 12, 9]
>>>
```

in the second example we will remove element 1. Recall that element 1 is the second element in the list.

```
>>> x
[8, 5, 12, 9]
>>> x.pop(1)   # remove element 1
5
>>> x   # print the list
[8, 12, 9]
>>>
```

remove()
Remove will delete the first occurrence of the given value in a list. If the element does not occur in the list then a value error is returned.

syntax
> `<list>.remove(<element>)`

Where `<list>` is the list with the elements
> `<element>` is the element to be removed from the list

Example:

```
>>> x=[8,5,12,9]
>>> x
[8, 5, 12, 9]
>>> x.remove(5)
>>> x
[8, 12, 9]
>>>
```

After `x.remove(5)`, 5 is removed from the list.

reverse()
reverse() will reverse the elements in a list, that is first element become last, second become next to last ... last element becomes first.

syntax
> `<list>.reverse()`

Where `<list>` is the list to be reversed

Example:

```
>>> x
[8, 5, 12, 9]
>>> x.reverse()   # reverse the elements in place
>>> x
[9, 12, 5, 8]
>>>
```

index()

Index() will return the position of the first occurrence of the given value. Index() will return a value error if the value does not exist in the list.

syntax

```
<list>.index(<element>)
```

Where `<list>` is the list to be searched
 `<element>` is the value whose position we are interested in.

Example:

```
>>> x
[8, 5, 12, 9]
>>> x.index(12)
2
>>>
```

6.7   List Methods

len()

In 3.2.3 we discussed the `len()` operator and used it to find the length of a string, we explained that this can be used on any collection of objects. It is worth pointing out that we can use the `len()` operator to find out the number of elements in a list.

Example

```
>>> x
['Lee', 'Adam', 'Peter', 'Clive']
>>> len(x)
4
>>>
```

In operator

The in operator discussed on 3.3 will test if an object is a member of a collection.

Example

```
>>> x
['Lee', 'Adam', 'Peter', 'Clive']
>>> 'Lee' in x
True
>>>
```

We will discuss two additional operators that can be used with list namely `min()` and `max()`.

min()

The `min()` operator will return the smallest value in the list.

syntax

   `min(<list>)`

Where `<list>` is the list that we want to find the smallest element of.

Example:

```
>>> x
['Lee', 'Adam', 'Peter', 'Clive']
>>> min(x)   # return the smallest value of x
'Adam'
>>> y
[5, 6, 7]
>>> min(y) #return the smallest value of y
5
>>>
```

Notice that `min()` will compare both strings and numeric data type.

max()

The `max()` operator will return the largest value in the list.

syntax

   `max(<list>)`

Where `<list>` is the list that we want to find the largest element of.

Example:

```
>>> x
['Lee', 'Adam', 'Peter', 'Clive']
>>> max(x)    #return the largest value
'Peter'
>>> y
[5, 6, 7]
>>> max(y)    #return the largest value
7
>>>
```

Practice Exercise 6

1. Given the list **bank_holidays_in_month = [1, 0, 1, 1, 2, 0, 0, 1, 0, 0, 0, 2]** where each element represent the number of bank holiday in a month, for example in January there is 1, in February 0, March there is 1etc. Write a function called **bank_holiday()**, that takes a number to represent the month and return the number of bank holidays in that month. Example: **bank_holiday(5) → 2**

2. Without using the sort(), function that is defined on list. Write a function called my_sort(), that takes an unsorted list and return the sorted list

3. Define a function called add_hello(), that takes any list and append the word "hello", to the list.

4. Define a function called **discount_ten()**, that takes a list of floating point number and return a list with each element having a ten percent discount.

5. Define a function called **remove_five()**, that takes a list as input and remove all occurrence of 5 in the list. Write the function in such a way that you will not receive an error if there is no 5s in the list.

6. A word is a palindrome if it reads the same thing in both directions. For example "civic", "radar", "level", "redder", "madam" are all palindrome. Write a function called is_palindrome(), that takes a word and return True if the word is a palindrome or False otherwise.

7. Define a function called **unique_elements()** that takes a list and return a list that only contain unique elements. The program should take repeated elements but only return one value of the element. Example in the list [1,2,2,3,3,4] it should return the list [1,2,3,4]

8. Define a function called **backways()**, that takes a list and return the list in reverse order.

9. Define a function called **sum_list()**, that takes a list as input and return the sum of all the elements in the list.

10. Define a function called mean_list(), that takes a list as input and returns the mean of the list. The mean is the sum of all the elements divided by the number of elements, you can use the function above defined in question 9.

11. Define a function called list_of_deviation(), that takes list as input and return a list that represent how much each element deviate from the mean.

12. Define a function called standard_deviation() that returns the standard deviation of a list. Feel free to use the functions defined in questions 10 and 11 above. We can use the following steps to find standard deviation:
    a. Find the mean
    b. List of deviation
    c. Squares of the deviation
    d. Sum of the squares of deviation
    e. Divided by one less than the number of items
    f. Square root of this number → use sqrt(), which is defined in the math module

Example of how to calculate standard deviation:

Given [1, 4, 5, 7, 9, 20]
Mean (1+4+6+8+9+20)/6 = 8
List of deviations [-7, -4, -2, 0, 1, 12]
Squares of the deviation [49, 16, 4, 0, 1, 144]
Sum of the squares of the deviation = 214
Divided by one less than the number of items in the list 214/5 = 42.8
Now the square root of 42.8 = 6.54
Standard deviation is about 6.54

Chapter 7 : Dictionary

What we will learn:

- How to create a dictionary
- How delete a key : value pair in a dictionary
- How to create a list of all the keys and values in a dictionary

Keywords

- Dictionary
- Keys
- Values

```
Python 3.3.0 (v3.3.0:bd8afb90ebf2, Sep 29 2012, 10:57:17) [MSC v.1600 64
D64)] on win32
Type "copyright", "credits" or "license()" for more information.
>>> bbc_radio_listeners={'Radio 1':11.8, 'Radio 2':14.5, 'Radio 3':2.3}
>>> bbc_radio_listeners
{'Radio 1': 11.8, 'Radio 2': 14.5, 'Radio 3': 2.3}
>>> bbc_radio_listeners['Radio 2']
14.5
>>> list(bbc_radio_listeners.keys())
['Radio 1', 'Radio 2', 'Radio 3']
>>> list(bbc_radio_listeners.values())
[11.8, 14.5, 2.3]
```

Subject Content	Learning Outcomes
3.1.2 Structures • How data types can be combined to make data structures • How data structures can make coding a solution to a problem simpler	• Be able to explain what a data structure is. • Be able to produce their own data structure that go beyond the built in structure of the language they are using. • Understand and be able to explain why data structures can make coding a solution simpler.

7.1 Definition

Dictionary is an important data structure provided in python. You can think of dictionary as a set of unordered pair using a key : value relationship, where a key is mapped to a value.

The key can be any immutable data type and therefore string and numbers are often used as keys. A list cannot be used as a key as list is mutable and can be changed using functions such as pop(), append() and others.

syntax
```
<variable> = {<key>:<value>, <key>:<value>, ...}
```

Where `<variable>` is the name of the dictionary following the same rule as declaring a variable in python.

`<key>` is an immutable data type in python.

`<value>` is an data to be stored in the dictionary.

Example:
```
>>> bbc_radio_listeners={'Radio 1':11.8, 'Radio 2':14.5, 'Radio 3':2.3, 'Radio 4':10.8}
>>> bbc_radio_listeners
{'Radio 4': 10.8, 'Radio 3': 2.3, 'Radio 2': 14.5, 'Radio 1': 11.8}
>>> bbc_radio_listeners['Radio 2']
14.5
>>>
```

From the above we notice that the dictionary is indexed by the key and not numbers as is the case with list from the previous chapter.

Secondly the pairs are not ordered but are stored in random order.

7.2 Modifying values in a dictionary

```
>>> bbc_radio_listeners['Radio 2'] = 9.6
>>> bbc_radio_listeners
{'Radio 4': 10.8, 'Radio 3': 2.3, 'Radio 2': 9.6, 'Radio 1': 11.8}
>>>
```

Keys are unique in each dictionary, and therefore assigning 9.6 to the key "Radio 2" will result in over writing the previous value that was stored in "Radio 2".

7.2.1 Deleting Entries

```
>>> del bbc_radio_listeners['Radio 2']
>>> bbc_radio_listeners
{'Radio 4': 10.8, 'Radio 3': 2.3, 'Radio 1': 11.8}
>>>
```

del will remove the key:value pair from the dictionary. Using del with a key that does not exist in the dictionary will result in a keyError.

7.3 List of keys and values

The keys() method will return a dictionary list, we can use the keys() and lists() method to return a list consisting of all the keys from the dictionary.

```
>>> bbc_radio_listeners
{'Radio 4': 10.8, 'Radio 3': 2.3, 'Radio 1': 11.8}
>>> list(bbc_radio_listeners.keys())
['Radio 4', 'Radio 3', 'Radio 1']
```

The values() method will return the values in the dictionary.

```
>>> bbc_radio_listeners
{'Radio 4': 10.8, 'Radio 3': 2.3, 'Radio 1': 11.8}
>>> list(bbc_radio_listeners.values())
[10.8, 2.3, 11.8]
>>>
```

The list will be unsorted; we can use the sorted method to sort the list.

```
>>> sorted(list(bbc_radio_listeners.values()))
[2.3, 10.8, 11.8]
>>>
```

Practice Exercise 7

1. Define a dictionary called **Football_managers** that store the name of the following football team and their manager.

Keys	Values
Manchester United	Alex Ferguson
Arsenal	Arsene Wenger
Everton	David Moyes
Norwich City	Chris Hughton

2. Add a new entry to the dictionary defined in question 1, with the following information Key= Chelsea and Value = Rafael Benitez. Print the new dictionary to the screen

3. Use the keys() method to create a list of all the keys in the dictionary, print this to the screen.

4. Use the values() method to create a list of all the values in the dictionary, print this to the screen.

5. Given the table below, create a dictionary that uses the key as year and a list as values, the list should consist of Bond Actor, Movie, Salary of actor and Box Office takings

Year	Bond Actor	Movie	Salary of actor (Millons)	Box Office takings (Millions)
2008	Daniel Craig	Quantom of Solace	8.9	514.2
2006	Daniel Craig	Casino Royale	3.4	581.5
2002	Pierce Brosnan	Die Another Day	16.5	465.4

6. Add another entry for the 2002 movie titled "The world is not enough". You can find the data at http://en.wikipedia.org/wiki/List_of_James_Bond_films .

7. Use the keys() method to create a list of all the keys in the dictionary, print this to the screen.

8. Use the values() method to create a list of all the values in the dictionary, print this to the screen.

Chapter 8 : Working With Files

What we will learn:
- How to open files in Pyton
- Syntax for manipulating files
- Creating a database
- Making queries

Keywords
- File
- Absolute path
- Relative path
- Database
- Query
- SQL

```
olympic_games - Notepad
File  Edit  Format  View  Help
This is Line 1
Here is a list of cities for multiple olympic games
London 1908, 1948, 2012
Athens 1896, 2004
Paris 1900, 1924
Los Angeles 1932, 1984
```

Subject Content	Learning Outcomes
3.1.7 Handling External Data • Using text files to read/write data • Using databases to read/write data	• Know how to an external text file to read and write data in a way that is appropriate for the programming language(s) used and the problem being solved. • Know how to read and write data from an external database in a way that is appropriate for the programming language(s) used and the problem being solved.

Files are used to store data on a secondary storage device. All the data that we have been using so far are data that disappears when we stop running the program. In order to have persistent data we have to store them on a secondary storage medium. This data can be used after the running program exit or whenever we wish to do so.

In python we use the *open()* function which is a built in function to open a file.

syntax
```
<variable_name> = open(<filename>, <mode>)
```

Where `<variable_name>` is a file object and will be used to refer to the opened file.

`<filename>` is the name of the file and extension. If the file is stored in the same directory as the running program then the name of the file is enough, otherwise the full file path is required which can be relative or absolute, we will discuss these later.

`<mode>` refers to the possible operations on the opened file. The possible modes are summarized in the table below.

Table 4

Mode	Meaning
'r'	Open for reading (default)
'w'	Open for writing. If the file exist python will delete all the contents first, if the file does not exist python will create a new file.
'x'	Create a new file and open it for writing
'a'	Open for writing, appending to the end of the file if it exists
'b'	Binary mode
't'	Text mode (default)
'+'	Open a disk file for updating (reading and writing)
'U'	Universal newline mode (for backward compatibility)

Example:
```
#Open the file in write mode
text_file = open("olympic_games.txt", "w")
```

Will create a text file called `Olympic_games.txt` in the current working directory, or if the file exist will truncate (delete all the contents) the file and open the file ready to be written to. `text_file` is the file handler stream created in the program, that we will use to refer to and access the file on disk.

8.1 Writing to a file

We use the write() function to write contents to a file.

```
print("Writing to a text file with the write() method")

#Open the file in write mode
text_file = open("olympic_games.txt", "w")

text_file.write("This is Line 1\n")
text_file.write("Here is a list of cities for multiple olympic games \n")
text_file.write("London 1908, 1948, 2012 \n")
text_file.write("Athens 1896, 2004 \n")
text_file.write("Paris 1900, 1924 \n")
text_file.write("Los Angeles 1932, 1984 \n")

text_file.close()
```

The code snippet above will create a new file or open an existing file called Olympic_games.txt, write some information to the file then close the file. A few things are worth noting here.

- "w" mode will either create a new file or open an existing one and delete all the contents
- write() invoked on the file handler will write the file
- \n is an escape sequence used to create newline in text files
- close() invoked on the file handler will close the current opened file. It is always a good idea to close files when you are no longer using them.

The following text file can be viewed in the current working directory.

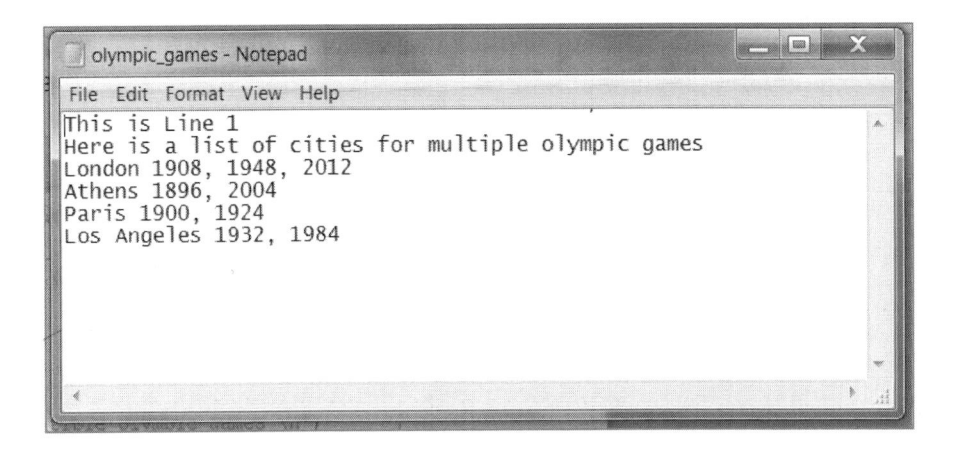

```
olympic_games - Notepad
File Edit Format View Help
This is Line 1
Here is a list of cities for multiple olympic games
London 1908, 1948, 2012
Athens 1896, 2004
Paris 1900, 1924
Los Angeles 1932, 1984
```

Notice that the name of the file is *olympic_games* which is the name supplied in the program code. The \n inserts new line in the document.

85

8.2 Printing a file to the screen

We use the *read()* function to read data from a file that is open in read mode and the *print()* function to print data in the file handler to the screen.

```
#now open the file and print to the screen
text_file = open("olympic_games.txt", "r")
print(text_file.read())

text_file.close()
```

The snippet above will first close the open stream, then re-open the stream, this time for reading. It will then use the read() function to read the stream and print the contents to the screen using the print() function. Finally we close the stream.

The entire script and output is repeated below.

The Script

```
# Creating a file and writing to it using the write method

print("Writing to a text file with the write() method")

#Open the file in write mode
text_file = open("olympic_games.txt", "w")

text_file.write("This is Line 1\n")
text_file.write("Here is a list of cities for multiple olympic games \n")
text_file.write("London 1908, 1948, 2012 \n")
text_file.write("Athens 1896, 2004 \n")
text_file.write("Paris 1900, 1924 \n")
text_file.write("Los Angeles 1932, 1984 \n")

text_file.close()

#now open the file and print to the screen
text_file = open("olympic_games.txt", "r")
print(text_file.read())

text_file.close()
```

The Output

```
>>> ============================== RESTART ==============================
>>>
Writing to a text file with the write() method
This is Line 1
Here is a list of cities for multiple olympic games
London 1908, 1948, 2012
Athens 1896, 2004
Paris 1900, 1924
Los Angeles 1932, 1984
```

The Text File

This text file will be created and saved in the current working directory.

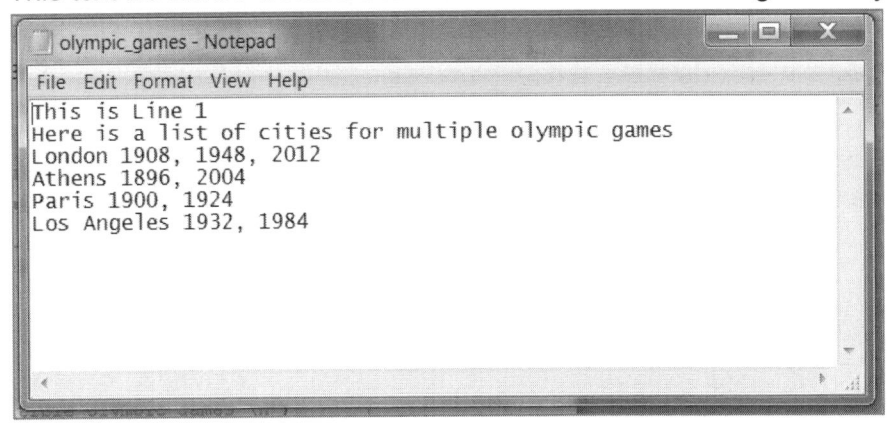

```
olympic_games - Notepad
File  Edit  Format  View  Help
This is Line 1
Here is a list of cities for multiple olympic games
London 1908, 1948, 2012
Athens 1896, 2004
Paris 1900, 1924
Los Angeles 1932, 1984
```

Note that text files take text (string) as input and therefore in order to write other data types to a text file they will first have to be converted to string. The *str()* function becomes very handy.

8.3   Appending a file

To add data to a file without deleting what is already there we open the file in append mode.

```python
#First open the file in append mode
text_file = open("olympic_games.txt", "a")

# Now we add the winter games host to the file
text_file.write("\n\nWinter Olympics\n")
text_file.write("Lake Placid 1932, 1980\n")
text_file.write("Innsbruck 1964, 1976\n")
text_file.write("St. Moritz 1928, 1948\n")

#Now close the file
text_file.close()
```

The code above will open the file in append mode and add the winter Olympic cities that host the games more than once. Again we close the file after using it. We can then re-open the file and print the contents to the screen. We should see both sets of information in the file and if we open the text file on our computer we should see the updated text file as seen below.

87

```
olympic_games - Notepad
File Edit Format View Help
This is Line 1
Here is a list of cities for multiple olympic games
London 1908, 1948, 2012
Athens 1896, 2004
Paris 1900, 1924
Los Angeles 1932, 1984

Winter Olympics
Lake Placid 1932, 1980
Innsbruck 1964, 1976
St. Moritz 1928, 1948
```

8.4 File Path

A **directory structure (folder structure)** is the way in which an operating system displays its files to the user. The Windows operating system uses drives names (typically identified by a letter) to denote the root directory or folder. The directory separator is the "\" (backslash) seen while the Unix based operating system uses the "/" (forward slash) as its directory separator. A file name is therefore the unique address given to identify a file. There are two ways of stating a file name using the address, 1) relative path and 2) absolute path.

In the previous section we used relative file path to open files. Relative file path start by using the current directory, therefore by running the code, python will create or open a file called *sample.txt* from the current working directory.

```
>>> new_file = open("sample.txt", "w")
```

The current working directory is the folder that the running program is operating in. We can find out the current working directory by using the function *getcwd()*. The function is a part of the OS module and therefore we will have to import this module before we can use the function. The following code will print the path of the current working directory:

```
>>> import os
>>> print(os.getcwd())
C:\Users\Devz\PythonExercise
>>>
```

To create the file at some other location we could use the absolute file path, where we give the full address, for example

```
>>> new_file = open("C:\\Users\\Devz\\PythonExercise\\sample.txt", "w")
>>>
```

Will open or create a file called sample.txt in the specified location *C:\Users\Devz\PythonExercise*, it is worth mentioning that in the command above we use double backslash to denote one backslash, the reason for this is that "\" denotes an escape sequence in python therefore we use two backslashes for a backslash. Alternatively we could proceed the file path with "r". File paths such as *C:\Users\Devz\PythonExercise* is called absolute file path, the difference is that the address is given from the topmost folder on the drive.

```
>>> new_file = open(r"C:\Users\Devz\PythonExercise\sample.txt", "w")
>>>
```

8.5 Working with Databases

A database is a collection of tables that store data. The software that operates on this data is called a database management system (DBMS). Most databases will contain more than table, but queries, triggers and views; each table is identified by a unique name. Almost all organisations will store data and will use a database at some point. It is therefore important for us to write programs that can use data in a database and update a database. The most common operation carried out on a database is query. Query in its strictest sense is asking the database a question, and the database respond by providing all the data items that meet the criteria. Before we discuss queries it is important to explain some key database terminologies. For the illustration in the table below we will use a database with a table of students similar to what is used in schools.

Table 5

Name	Meaning	Example
Table	A collection of data relevant to one entity	A students table
Records	Collection of all the data on a single entity	001, John, Doe, 12/03/1992, 7S
Field	Single column of data in a table	John Benjamin Alex Ahmed Crystal Simon
Field Name	The name given to the field of	First Name

Here is an example of a table within a database with the sections labelled

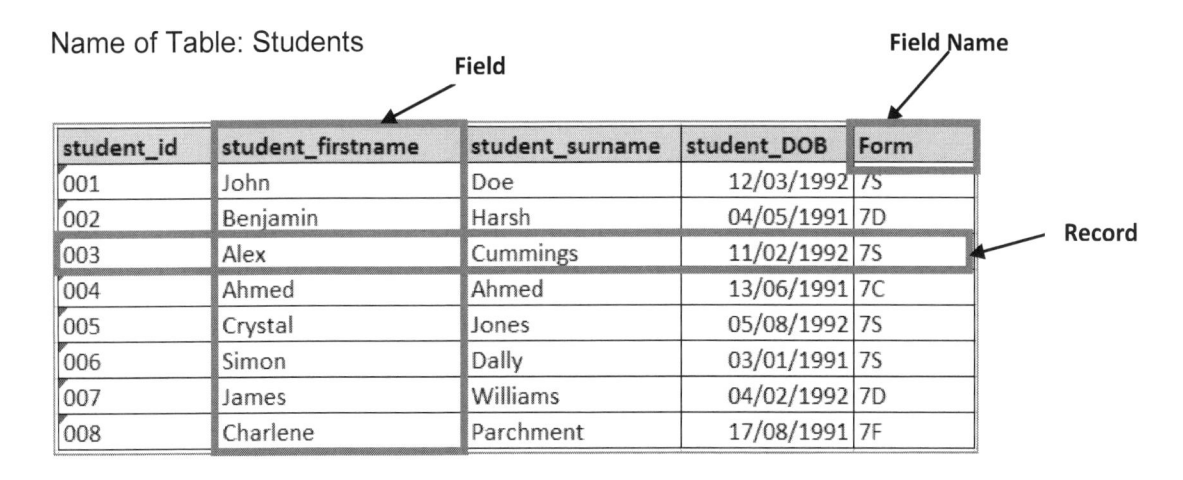

Name of Table: Students

student_id	student_firstname	student_surname	student_DOB	Form
001	John	Doe	12/03/1992	7S
002	Benjamin	Harsh	04/05/1991	7D
003	Alex	Cummings	11/02/1992	7S
004	Ahmed	Ahmed	13/06/1991	7C
005	Crystal	Jones	05/08/1992	7S
006	Simon	Dally	03/01/1991	7S
007	James	Williams	04/02/1992	7D
008	Charlene	Parchment	17/08/1991	7F

Each field in a data has a data type. The data types are similar to the ones discuss in chapter 4. The universal language used to create and manipulate databases is called structured query language (SQL pronounced sequel).

Some DBMS such as Microsoft Access will generate the SQL codes for the user. In order to use databases in python it is worth understanding some SQL commands, we will turn our attention to this.

8.6 SQL

We will discuss the following statements available in SQL:

- CREATE TABLE – *This will create a table in a database*
- SELECT – *Display data that is in a table in a database*
- UPDATE – *change data in a table in a database*
- DELETE – *remove data from a table in a database*
- INSERT INTO – *insert new data into a table in a database*

8.6.1 The CREATE TABLE Statement

We first use the CREATE TABLE statement to create the table that we will be using as a running example.

syntax
```
CREATE TABLE <table_name>
(
<field_name> <data_type>,
<field_name> <data_type>,
<field_name> <data_type>
)
```

Where `<table_name>` is the name of the table to be created in the database
`<field_name>` is the name of the column to be created in the table
`<data_type>` is the data type of the column

Example:

```
CREATE TABLE Students
(
student_id text,
student_firstname text,
student_surname text,
student_DOB date,
Form text
)
```

Will create the following table called Students in the database

student_id	student_firstname	student_surname	student_DOB	Form

For the rest of the SQL section we will use the following table as our running example

student_id	student_firstname	student_surname	student_DOB	Form
001	John	Doe	12/03/1992	7S
002	Benjamin	Harsh	04/05/1991	7D
003	Alex	Cummings	11/02/1992	7S
004	Ahmed	Ahmed	13/06/1991	7C
005	Crystal	Jones	05/08/1992	7S
006	Simon	Dally	03/01/1991	7S
007	James	Williams	04/02/1992	7D
008	Charlene	Parchment	17/08/1991	7F

8.6.2 The SELECT Statement

The SELECT statement is used to display data in a table. We can view all the data or we can specify a criterion in which case only data that is meeting the criteria will be displayed.

syntax
```
SELECT <field_name> FROM <table_name>
```

Where `<field_name>` is the name of the column to be selected and
`<table_name>` is the name of the table in the database

Example:

```
SELECT student_firstname FROM Students
```

Will produce the following output

student_firstname
John
Benjamin
Alex
Ahmed
Crystal
Simon
James
Charlene

```
SELECT student_firstname, student_surname FROM Students
```

Will produce the following output

student_firstname	student_surname
John	Doe
Benjamin	Harsh
Alex	Cummings
Ahmed	Ahmed
Crystal	Jones
Simon	Dally
James	Williams
Charlene	Parchment

The wildcard (*) is a quick way of selecting all columns in the table and therefore

```
SELECT * FROM Students
```

Will produce the entire table

student_id	student_firstname	student_surname	student_DOB	Form
001	John	Doe	12/03/1992	7S
002	Benjamin	Harsh	04/05/1991	7D
003	Alex	Cummings	11/02/1992	7S
004	Ahmed	Ahmed	13/06/1991	7C
005	Crystal	Jones	05/08/1992	7S
006	Simon	Dally	03/01/1991	7S
007	James	Williams	04/02/1992	7D
008	Charlene	Parchment	17/08/1991	7F

8.6 The WHERE Clause

The "Where" clause is used in conjunction with the select statement; this is used to specify a criteria in the selection.

syntax
```
SELECT <field_name> FROM <table_name>
WHERE <field_name> operator <value>
```

Where `<field_name>` is the name of the column to be selected and
`<table_name>` is the name of the table in the database
`operator` is any operator from the table below
`<value>` is any legal value that can be stored in the field name selected

Table 6

Operator	Meaning
=	Equal to
<> or !=	Not equal to
<	Less than
>	Greater than
<=	Less than or equal to
>=	Greater than or equal to
BETWEEN	Value between a given range including the bounds
LIKE	Matches a given pattern
IN	To find more than one value in a column

Example:

```
SELECT * FROM Students
WHERE Form='7S'
```

Will produce

student_id	student_firstname	student_surname	student_DOB	Form
001	John	Doe	12/03/1992	7S
003	Alex	Cummings	11/02/1992	7S
005	Crystal	Jones	05/08/1992	7S
006	Simon	Dally	03/01/1991	7S

Notice that '7S' requires single quotation as the data type is text, there is no need for quotation of the data type is numeric.

8.6.4 *The UPDATE Statement*

This statement is used to change records by updating them in a table in a database.

syntax

```
UPDATE <table_name>
SET <column1> = value1, <column2>=value2, ...
WHERE <field_name> = value
```

Where `<table_name>` is the name of the table in the database
`<column1>` is the first column to be updated
`<column2>` is the second column to be updated
`<field_name>` specify the specific record to be updated

Note that the WHERE clause specify the particular record to be updated. If this is left blank, then all the record will be updated.

Example:

```
UPDATE Students
SET Form = '7S'
WHERE student_firstname='Charlene'
```

Before the update

student_id	student_firstname	student_surname	student_DOB	Form
001	John	Doe	12/03/1992	7S
002	Benjamin	Harsh	04/05/1991	7D
003	Alex	Cummings	11/02/1992	7S
004	Ahmed	Ahmed	13/06/1991	7C
005	Crystal	Jones	05/08/1992	7S
006	Simon	Dally	03/01/1991	7S
007	James	Williams	04/02/1992	7D
008	Charlene	Parchment	17/08/1991	7F

After the update statement

student_id	student_firstname	student_surname	student_DOB	Form
001	John	Doe	12/03/1992	7S
002	Benjamin	Harsh	04/05/1991	7D
003	Alex	Cummings	11/02/1992	7S
004	Ahmed	Ahmed	13/06/1991	7C
005	Crystal	Jones	05/08/1992	7S
006	Simon	Dally	03/01/1991	7S
007	James	Williams	04/02/1992	7D
008	Charlene	Parchment	17/08/1991	7S

Notice that the Charlene is now in form 7S.

8.6.5 The DELETE Statement

This statement is used to remove records from a database.

syntax
```
DELETE FROM <table_name>
WHERE <field_name> = value
```

Where `<table_name>` is the name of the table in the database
`<field_name> = value` specify the specific record to be deleted

Example:

```
DELETE FROM Students
WHERE student_firstname='Charlene'
```

Before the delete statement

student_id	student_firstname	student_surname	student_DOB	Form
001	John	Doe	12/03/1992	7S
002	Benjamin	Harsh	04/05/1991	7D
003	Alex	Cummings	11/02/1992	7S
004	Ahmed	Ahmed	13/06/1991	7C
005	Crystal	Jones	05/08/1992	7S
006	Simon	Dally	03/01/1991	7S
007	James	Williams	04/02/1992	7D
008	Charlene	Parchment	17/08/1991	7F

After the delete statement

student_id	student_firstname	student_surname	student_DOB	Form
001	John	Doe	12/03/1992	7S
002	Benjamin	Harsh	04/05/1991	7D
003	Alex	Cummings	11/02/1992	7S
004	Ahmed	Ahmed	13/06/1991	7C
005	Crystal	Jones	05/08/1992	7S
006	Simon	Dally	03/01/1991	7S
007	James	Williams	04/02/1992	7D

8.6.6   *The INSERT INTO Statement*

The insert into statement is used to insert a new record into a database

syntax
```
INSERT INTO <table_name> (column1, coulmn2, column3, ...)
VALUES (value1, value2, value3, ...)
```

Where `<table_name>` is the name of the table in the database
  `column` is the column to where the value should be inserted into and
  `value` is the value to be inserted into the matching column

Not that the column is optional, but SQL will insert the values in consecutive columns if they are omitted. Specifying the column is a good way to insert data into non-consecutive columns.

Example:

```
INSERT INTO Students
VALUES ('009', 'Paul', 'Piggot', '15/07/1992', '7C')
```

Before the insert into statement

student_id	student_firstname	student_surname	student_DOB	Form
001	John	Doe	12/03/1992	7S
002	Benjamin	Harsh	04/05/1991	7D
003	Alex	Cummings	11/02/1992	7S
004	Ahmed	Ahmed	13/06/1991	7C
005	Crystal	Jones	05/08/1992	7S
006	Simon	Dally	03/01/1991	7S
007	James	Williams	04/02/1992	7D
008	Charlene	Parchment	17/08/1991	7F

After the insert into statement

student_id	student_firstname	student_surname	student_DOB	Form
001	John	Doe	12/03/1992	7S
002	Benjamin	Harsh	04/05/1991	7D
003	Alex	Cummings	11/02/1992	7S
004	Ahmed	Ahmed	13/06/1991	7C
005	Crystal	Jones	05/08/1992	7S
006	Simon	Dally	03/01/1991	7S
007	James	Williams	04/02/1992	7D
008	Charlene	Parchment	17/08/1991	7S
009	Paul	Piggot	15/07/1992	7C

We could have used the field name to specify the columns where we want the data to be inserted, but in this case, we want to insert in all columns and therefore it is not necessary.

8.7 SQL and Python

Python provide the *sqlite3* library to manipulate lightweight disk databases. Before we try to create or use a database we first have to import the sqlite3 library. We use the keyword import for this. This is demonstrated below.

```
#we first import the sqlite3 library
import sqlite3
```

Connect

Now that the sqlite3 library is imported we can connect to and use a database. Similar to files, before we use a database we need to have a handler in our program that interact with the physical database on disk or in RAM. We use the connect() function as defined in the sqlite3 library, This function will open a connection to the SQLite database file. The following code snippet will connect to a database called school.

```python
#we first import the sqlite3 library
import sqlite3

#Create a handler called new_db that connects to db on disk
new_db = sqlite3.connect('C:\\Users\\Devz\\PythonExercise\\school.db')
```

The argument to the function is the file path for the database, notice that we use double backslash '\\' in our file path seen that single backslash denote an escape sequence.

Create Cursor Object

In python the Cursor object allows us to work with and manipulate databases. To create a cursor object we call the cursor method on the connection object. In our example the connection object is new_db, we will create a new cursor called c.

```python
#we first import the sqlite3 library
import sqlite3

#Create a handler called new_db that connects to db on disk
new_db = sqlite3.connect('C:\\Users\\Devz\\PythonExercise\\school.db')

#Create a new cursor object to manipulate the database
c=new_db.cursor()
```

Now that we have a connection to our database and a cursor object we can execute SQL statements to create our table and insert data into our tables. We will create a table called students with the same properties as before.

Create table
We first create a table.
```python
#Now create a table called Students
c.execute('''CREATE TABLE Students
(student_id text,
student_firstname text,
student_surname text,
student_DOB date,
Form text)
''')
```
Notice that we are using SQL commands to create the table.

Use INSERT INTO Statement to populate the table
Next we use the INSERT INTO statement to insert values into our table
```python
#insert data into our table
c.execute('''INSERT INTO Students
        VALUES ('001', 'John', 'Doe', '12/03/1992', '7S')''')
```

Notice that we are using the version where we do not specify the field names seen that we will be inserting into all columns.

Commit and Close

We use the commit() statement to save/commit the final transaction, and finally close the database.

```
#Save changes using the commit() function
new_db.commit()

#Close the connection to the database
new_db.close()
```

Putting all the codes together:

```
#we first import the sqlite3 library

import sqlite3

#Create a handler called new_db that connects to db on disk
new_db = sqlite3.connect('C:\\Users\\Devz\\PythonExercise\\school.db')

#Create a new cursor object to manipulate the database
c=new_db.cursor()

#Now create a table called Students
c.execute('''CREATE TABLE Students
(student_id text,
student_firstname text,
student_surname text,
student_DOB date,
Form text)
''')

#insert data into our table
c.execute('''INSERT INTO Students
        VALUES ('001', 'John', 'Doe', '12/03/1992', '7S')''')

#Save changes using the commit() function
new_db.commit()

#Close the connection to the database
new_db.close()
```

After executing this code the database called school.db will be created in the specified location (C:\Users\Devz\PythonExercise\school.db), with a table called Students and record inserted.

student_id	student_firstname	student_surname	student_DOB	Form
001	John	Doe	12/03/1992	7S

The physical files are shown below. Note that this file is not readable by normal programs on the computer, and therefore if we open this file we will see symbols.

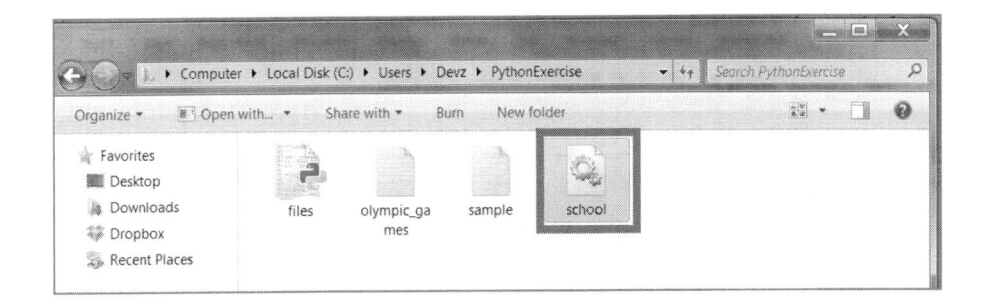

We can however use python to read the data from this file and print this data to the screen. The following code snippet re-connects to the database, reads the file and prints the data to the screen.

```
#Re-connect to the database
new_db=sqlite3.connect('C:\\Users\\Devz\\PythonExercise\\school.db')

#Create a cursor object
c=new_db.cursor()

#Use the SELECT statement with wildcard to select all columns
c.execute("SELECT * FROM Students")

#use the fetchone function to fetch one row of data
row=c.fetchone()

#print the row to the screen
print(row)

#Finally close the connection
new_db.close()
```

The result of executing this code is

```
>>> ============================== RESTART ==================================
>>>
('001', 'John', 'Doe', '12/03/1992', '7S')
>>>
```

It is always good practice to close the database connection once you are finish using the database, as other processes will not be able to access the opened database.

Here are some other functions defined on the object cursor and a description of what they do.

executemany(...)
    Repeatedly execute a SQL statement

executescript(...)
    Executes a multiple SQL statements at once

fethchall(...)
    Fetches all rows from the resultset

fethchmany(...)
    fetch several rows from the result set.

Practice Exercise 8

1. Create a text file in the current working directory that create and store the text file that shows a list of the last five (5) prime ministers of the United Kingdom as shown below.

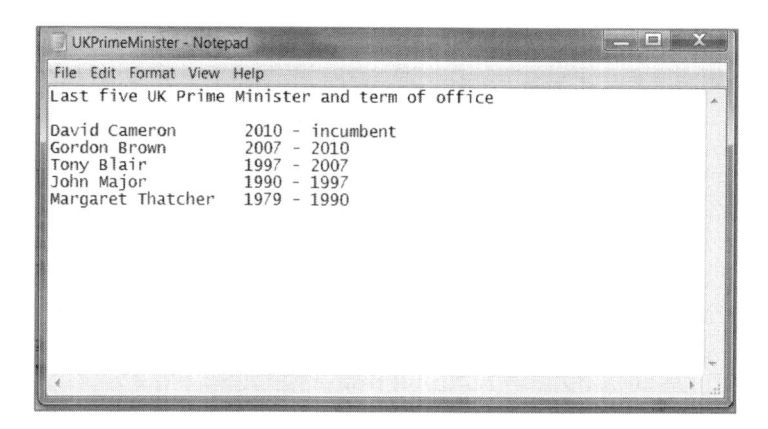

   ```
   UKPrimeMinister - Notepad
   File  Edit  Format  View  Help
   Last five UK Prime Minister and term of office

   David Cameron       2010 - incumbent
   Gordon Brown        2007 - 2010
   Tony Blair          1997 - 2007
   John Major          1990 - 1997
   Margaret Thatcher   1979 - 1990
   ```

   a. Now write a python program that will read the file called "UKPrimeMinister.txt", that was created above and print the content to the screen. The output is shown below.

   ```
   >>> ============================ RESTART ============================
   >>>
   Writing text file
   Last five UK Prime Minister and term of office

   David Cameron       2010 - incumbent
   Gordon Brown        2007 - 2010
   Tony Blair          1997 - 2007
   John Major          1990 - 1997
   Margaret Thatcher   1979 - 1990

   >>>
   ```

2. The code below should create a text file called "my_quote.txt". The function update_file() is defined to take a file name and a string containing a quote. The function should open the file called "my_quote.txt", and update it with a new quote. The program should prompt the user to enter a quote three times. Then print the contents of the file to the screen. At the moment there are two things wrong with the code.
   1) only the last quote is save in the file.
   2) The user is being prompted four times instead of three

   Examine the code and correct the code to get the desired outcome.

100

Desired outcome

```
>>> =============================== RESTART ===============================
>>>
Enter your favourite quote: Education is the most powerful weapon which you can use to chang the world, Nelson Mandela
Enter your favourite quote: Education is not preparation for life it is life itself, John Dewey
Enter your favourite quote: The only thing that interferes with my learning is my education, Albert Einstein
This is an update
Education is the most powerful weapon which you can use to chang the world, Nelson Mandela

This is an update
Education is not preparation for life it is life itself, John Dewey

This is an update
The only thing that interferes with my learning is my education, Albert Einstein

>>>
```

And Text file:

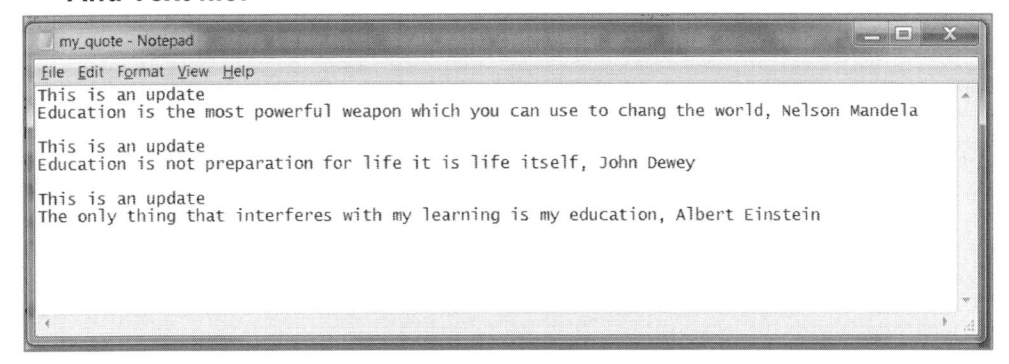

```
my_quote - Notepad
File Edit Format View Help
This is an update
Education is the most powerful weapon which you can use to chang the world, Nelson Mandela

This is an update
Education is not preparation for life it is life itself, John Dewey

This is an update
The only thing that interferes with my learning is my education, Albert Einstein
```

Code to be corrected:

```python
# update three quotes to a file

file_name = "my_quote.txt"
#create a file called my_quote.txt
new_file = open(file_name, 'w')
new_file.close()


def update_file(file_name, quote):
    #First open the file
    new_file = open(file_name, 'w')
    new_file.write("This is an update\n")
    new_file.write(quote)
    new_file.write("\n\n")

    #now close the file
    new_file.close()

for index in range(1,3):
    quote = input("Enter your favourite quote: ")
    update_file(file_name, quote)


# Now print the contents to the screen
new_file = open(file_name, 'r')
print(new_file.read())

# And finally close the file
new_file.close()
```

3. Complete the following code to create a database called "Library.db", that has a table called Books. The code should then populate the table with the following information.

book_isbn	book_title	book_type	book_author	publisher
978-0-340-88851-3	A2 Pure Mathematics	Non fictional	Catherine Berry	Hodder Education
978-1-118-10227-5	Android 4 Application Development	Non fictional	Reto Meier	Wiley
0-596-00699-3	Programming C#	Non fictional	Jesse Liberty	O Reilly

It should then print the snippet below back to the screen.

Incomplete Code

```python
#we first import the sqlite3 library
import sqlite3

#insert the correct path here
new_db = sqlite3.connect('C:')

#Create a new cursor object to manipulate the database
c=new_db.cursor()

#Now create a table called Students
c.execute('''CREATE TABLE Books
(book_isbn text,
book_title text,
book_type text,
book_author text,
publisher text)
''')
#insert Statements here to add data to the table


new_db.commit()

#Close the connection to the database
new_db.close()


#Re-connect to the database - insert the correct path
new_db=sqlite3.connect('C:')

#Create a cursor object
c=new_db.cursor()

#Use the SELECT statement to select all the data

#use the fetchone function to fetch one row of data
book_library=c.fetchall()

#print the row to the screen
for book in book_library:
    print(book)

#Finally close the connection
new_db.close()
```

4. Explain the effect of running the following code on a database

```
SELECT Product.Name, Product.Quantity, Product.Price
FROM Product
WHERE Product.Quantity > 20
```

102

Chapter 9 : Classes

What we will learn:

- Object Oriented Programming
- What is a class
- How to create a class
- Assigning values to a class

Keywords

- Object oriented
- Object
- Attributes
- Class
- Abstract Data Type

```
class Student:
    """ The Student class defines a student with
    attributes: name, age, form
    """
    #Attributes
    name = "not set"
    age = 1
    form = "?"

    #Functions
    def get_name(self):
        return self.name

    def get_age(self):
        return self.age

    def get_form(self):
        return self.form

    def set_name(self, new_name):
        self.name = new_name

    def set_age(self, new_age):
        self.age=new_age

    def set_form(self, new_form):
        self.form = new_form

    def say_hello(self):
        print("hello my name is", self.name, " I'm in form ", self.form)

#create a new Student
student1 = Student()

#Set the name of Student1 to John Doe
student1.set_name("John Doe")

#Use the accessor method to print the name
print(student1.get_name())
```

Subject Content	Learning Outcomes
3.1.2 Structures • How data types can be combined to make data structures • How data structures can make coding a solution to a problem simpler	• Be able to explain what a data structure is. • Be able to produce their own data structure that go beyond the built in structure of the language they are using. • Understand and be able to explain why data structures can make coding a solution simpler.

9.1 Object Oriented Programming (OOP)

We had a thorough discussion on data types in chapter 3. It turns out that most application in real life will require other data types that are not supplied with python. Luckily python provides the facility to create our own data type. New data types created are often referred to as objects; and the process is called object oriented programming. In chapter 0 when we introduced python, we stated that python was a hybrid language and supported multiple programming paradigm (a way of thinking about computation), it turns out that the ability to create classes and manipulate objects qualifies python to be an object oriented programming language. As an example let us consider a student enrolment system used at a school or university it would be a great idea if we could refer to a student and python understand that we are talking about a person who has a name, address, telephone number, is registered for certain courses, and can do things such as walk, run, take an exam to name a few. It turns out that these entities (student in this case) are referred to as objects.

An **object** is a thing or an event in our application. Objects can have data items, these are known as **attributes**. Objects also have behaviours which are called **methods**. Earlier in our student's example, we classified a student as an object. The diagram below shows the student object, with some attributes and behaviours:

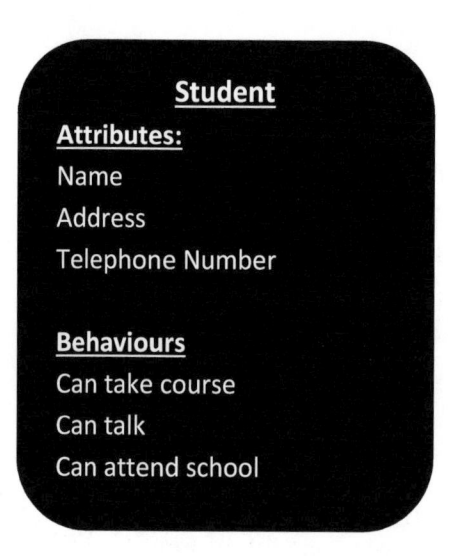

Student
Attributes:
Name
Address
Telephone Number

Behaviours
Can take course
Can talk
Can attend school

9.2 Why do we use classes?

1) **To bring the solution space closer to the problem space**. It is more natural to want to find out what is the name of a student than just referring to the string name. Computer programs are written to solve problems, Where the problem occur is referred to as the problem space, for example the problem space in our example above is in school and in particular in a course registration system. Since we are using the computer to solve this problem, then the solution space is in the computer. Using classes will give the programmer the ability to relate real life entities (students) to the interpreter, this bringing the solution space closer to the problem space.

2) **To develop so called abstract data type (ADT)**. Abstract data types are new data types that we can define numerous operations on. For example if we develop a new ADT called shapes we can define interesting methods such as draw_self(), or colour_self(), which allows the shape to draw and colour itself.

3) **For reuse of code.** If we have a definition of a good ADT, then we can always import that ADT and use the methods that are already defined. Let us say we developed the student registration system mentioned above and now we want to develop an extra-curricular club program that has students then there is no need to re-define the student ADT that was developed earlier. Furthermore other programmers can use ADT that was developed by other programmers.

4) **To enforce Data encapsulation.** Data encapsulation is information hiding. It turns out that with classes a programmer can use a new ADT without knowing the underlining implementation. This allows programmers to develop codes that other programmers can use, by accessing the methods that are defined over these ADTs without worrying about the intricacies of how this is actually accomplished. This also give the unique advantage where if a new way of accomplishing a task comes about then the writer of the ADT can make this change and the programmer using this code will not break. We have seen this modular design in engineering and mechanics before where the driver of a car is not necessarily concerned about how the pedal uses lever to connect to the master cylinder which in turn apply the disk pads to the wheel to stop the car. Instead he is only concerned with the fact that when he pushes on the brake pedal, this will have the effect of stopping the car. The designer of the car can choose whether to use drum brakes, air brakes, disc brakes or another braking system that is not discovered as yet; this will not affect the driver pushing on the pedal to stop the car. In a similar manner if a more efficient data structure arrive then the designer of the ADT can implement this and all programmers benefit without breaking any code.

9.3 Data types in Python

We have seen objects before. All data types in python are objects. The implementation of an object is called a class.

```
>>> name = 'Patrick'
>>> print(type(name))
<class 'str'>
>>>
>>> number = 45
>>> print(type(number))
<class 'int'>
>>>
>>> z = [1,2,3]
>>> print(type(z))
<class 'list'>
>>>
```

From the code snippet above, we assign "Patrick" to name, and when we print the type() then we see get <class 'str'>, this means that name is an instance of a string class. Similarly number is an instance of the integer class and z is an instance of the list class.

We have encountered string (a collection of characters) before. We also explored methods that are defined on string. Upper() and lower() are two of such methods. It turns out that every string has these methods defined on them, this is the case because in the definition of the string class, upper() and lower() is defined.

```
>>> month = 'September'
>>> print(month.upper())
SEPTEMBER
>>> #now print the lower case of month
>>> print(month.lower())
september
>>>
```

To view all the methods that are defined on an object we use the dir() method.

```
>>> dir(month)
['__add__', '__class__', '__contains__', '__delattr__', '__dir__', '__doc__', '__eq__', '__format__', '__ge__', '__getattribute__', '__getitem__', '__getnewargs__', '__gt__', '__hash__', '__init__', '__iter__', '__le__', '__len__', '__lt__', '__mod__', '__mul__', '__ne__', '__new__', '__reduce__', '__reduce_ex__', '__repr__', '__rmod__', '__rmul__', '__setattr__', '__sizeof__', '__str__', '__subclasshook__', 'capitalize', 'casefold', 'center', 'count', 'encode', 'endswith', 'expandtabs', 'find', 'format', 'format_map', 'index', 'isalnum', 'isalpha', 'isdecimal', 'isdigit', 'isidentifier', 'islower', 'isnumeric', 'isprintable', 'isspace', 'istitle', 'isupper', 'join', 'ljust', 'lower', 'lstrip', 'maketrans', 'partition', 'replace', 'rfind', 'rindex', 'rjust', 'rpartition', 'rsplit', 'rstrip', 'split', 'splitlines', 'startswith', 'strip', 'swapcase', 'title', 'translate', 'upper', 'zfill']
>>>
```

Notice that all of these methods are defined on all strings.

9.4 Defining a class

We use the class keyword followed by the name to define a class.

syntax
```
class <class_name>:
    'class_docstring'
    <class_suite>
```

Where `<class_name>` is the name of the class following the same conventions as naming variables, that was discussed in chapter 1.

`'class_docstring'` or documentation string is that explain what the class is about. This should give the user of the class enough information about the class being defined.

`<class_suite>` is the statements that define the class. This will contain the methods that define the class, and are invoked whenever we have instances of the class.

Example:

```
class Student:
    """ The Student class defines a student with
    attributes: name, age, form
    """
    #Attributes
    name = "not set"
    age = 1
    form = "7"

    #Functions
    def get_name(self):
        return self.name

    def get_age(self):
        return self.age

    def get_form(self):
        return self.form

    def set_name(self, new_name):
        self.name = new_name

    def set_age(self, new_age):
        self.age=new_age

    def set_form(self, new_form):
        self.form = new_form

    def say_hello(self):
        print("hello my name is", self.name, " I'm in form ", self.form)
```

The code snippet above will define the student class. The different sections are discussed below.

The class and docstring

```
class Student:
    """ The Student class defines a student with
    attributes: name, age, form
    """
```

The keyword class is used followed by the name of the class and colon.

The docstring or documentation string is used to build the documentation for any application that is using the class. This information also appears when we use the help facility to display the details of the Student class.

The Attributes

```
#Attributes
name = "not set"
age = 1
form = "7"
```

This is the section to list the attributes on the class and initialize the default values.

The class functions

```
#Functions
def get_name(self):
    return self.name

def get_age(self):
    return self.age

def get_form(self):
    return self.form

def set_name(self, new_name):
    self.name = new_name

def set_age(self, new_age):
    self.age=new_age

def set_form(self, new_form):
    self.form = new_form

def say_hello(self):
    print("hello my name is", self.name, " I'm in form ", self.form)
```

The class functions are used to access and change the attributes of the class. Notice the use of the word self. It turns out that we use self with the dot operator to refer to attributes of data items that belongs to the class.

9.4.1 Using the class

When we create a class, this is called an instance of the class. The following code will create an instance of student1 and use some of its functions.

```
#create a new Student
student1 = Student()

#Set the name of Student1 to John Doe
student1.set_name("John Doe")

#Use the accessor method to print the name
print(student1.get_name())

#Say hello from student1
print(student1.say_hello())
```

A few things to note above:
- We declare a variable and assign the name of the class as if it was a function.
- Once we create an instance of the class we can now use the class methods

This is the output that we would get.

```
>>> ================================ RESTART ================================
>>>
John Doe
hello my name is John Doe  I'm in form  7
None
>>>
```

Notice that if we create a new instance of the student class and say hello we will get a different message.

```
>>> student2 = Student()
>>> print(student2.say_hello())
hello my name is not set  I'm in form  7
None
>>>
```

When we say hello, the default values are displayed.

Practice Exercise 9

1. Create a class called Time with the following attributes, hour, minutes, and seconds. These should initialise to (12:00:00), unless the user supply another time. Create accessor functions with the following name and functionality.
    a. get_hour ()– return the current hour
    b. get_minute() – return the current minute
    c. get_second() – return the current second
    d. print_time() – print the current value of time

    e. And the following mutator function
    f. set_hour() – takes a new hour and set this as hour
    g. set_minute() – takes a new hour and set this as the minute
    h. set_seconds() – take a new second and set this as the second
    i. increment_second() – increment second by one second, note that if second is 59, incrementing will increment minute by one and turn seconds to 00.
    j. increment_minute() – increment minute by one, note that if the minute is at 59, incrementing minute will result in incrementing hour by one.
    k. increment_hour() – will result in incrementing hour by one, if hour is 12, this should return to 1.

2. Write a python program that inserts the time class, and create two instances of time, one with the default time and the other a user defined time. Use each of the accessor and mutator function, printing the values before and after the mutator function.

3. Create a class called Fraction, with the following attributes, numerator and denominator, these should initialize to (0/1), unless the user supply another fraction. Create accessor function called:
    a. get_numerator() – return the numerator
    b. get_denominator() – return the denominator
    c. print_fraction() – that prints the fraction
    d. print_type() – print the type of fraction ("proper" if the denominator is larger than the numerator, "improper" if the numerator is larger than the denominator)
    e. And the following mutator function
    f. set_numerator() – takes a new numerator and set this as numerator
    g. set_denominator() – takes a new denominator and set this as denominator
    h. inverse() – change the numerator to the denominator and vise versa, this should not change if the numerator is 0.

4. Write a python program that inserts the Fraction class, and create two instances of fraction, one with the default fraction and the other a user defined fraction. Use each of the accessor and mutator function, printing the values before and after the mutator function.

Chapter 10: Dealing With Errors

What we will learn:
- How to identify errors
- Categorize different types of errors
- How to fix different errors
- Examples of errors

Keywords
- Run-time errors
- Syntax
- Semantics
- Recursive
- Exceptions
- Errors

```
File  Edit  Format  Run  Options  Windows  Help
try:
    x=int(input("Enter a number: "))
except (ValueError, TypeError):
    print("Something went wrong")
else:
    print("Nothing went wrong")

#file will remain open if an exception is raised

try:
    test_file = open("example_file.txt", 'w')
    test_file.write("Some operations")
except IOError:
    print("File don't exist ...")
    test_file.close()
```

Subject Content	Learning Outcomes
3.1.6 Error handling - Different types of error that can occur - How to test your code for errors - How to detect errors from within code - How to recover from errors within the code	- Be able to discuss and identify the different types of errors that can occur within code (ie syntax, run-time, logical). - Understand that some errors can be detected and corrected during the coding stage. - Understand that some errors will occur during the execution of the code. - Know how to detect errors at execution time and how to handle those errors to prevent the program from crashing where desirable - Understand that computer programs can be developed with tools to help the programmer detect and deal with errors.

10.1 Exceptions and errors

There are different types of errors that can occur when we are writing programs. In this chapter we will discuss these and examine possible solutions.

Table 7

Types of errors

Type of Error	Meaning	Example

Syntax	A syntax error occurs when the programmer uses a token (letter, symbol, and operator) somewhere that is not defined in the grammar of the language.
	
	Programming languages have rules, similar to other form of communication. The interpreter takes the source code and parses the tokens then send this parsed byte code to the evaluator to get its meaning.
		`if age<18`
		`   print("Child")`
		
		Here the colon is missing after the condition (`age<18`)

Runtime	A runtime error occurs during execution of a program. The programmer normally thought about these but normally can do nothing about them. These are often dealt with by the exception handler.	Program running out of memory. Faulty hardware

Semantic or logical	Semantic refers to the meaning of the things. These errors happen because there are errors with the logic of the program, which gives unexpected results. The interpreter will not raise an exception or give an error message for semantic errors but the user will not get the expected result.
	
	In evaluating $\frac{15}{2\pi}$ in python we would type `15/2*math.pi` Seen that division and multiplication have the same precedence we would get 23.56, instead of the correct answer 2.38. In order to get the correct answer we would have to use brackets therefore, we would type `15/(2*math.pi)`
		For $\frac{12}{5\pi}$
		
		`12/5*math.pi`
		incorrect
		
		`12/(5*math.pi)`
		correct

In general the term **Exception** is used to describe when something goes wrong in a program, this include errors caused by the programmer and external factors such as hardware failure. Some programming languages make explicit differentiation between an error caused by a programmer and an exception. In python the difference is more subtle in that both errors and exception are handled by the BaseException class. Subclasses are then derived which are either errors or exceptions.

We will now turn our attention to dealing with these kind of errors and then to exceptions.

10.2   Syntax error

Syntax errors are quite easy to fix. The interpreter will raise this error where it notices that the error occurred. This is often at the exact location or sometimes in the previous line. For example if a token such as a closed bracket or a colon is missing from the previous line the syntax error is normally noticed and highlighted in the following line. The code snippet below demonstrates this.

```
>>> print("I am leaving out the closed bracket here"
      but when I run the program the error is in the wrong place

SyntaxError: invalid syntax
>>>
```

We will also get a syntax error if we group two operators together, for example

```
>>> 5 + 4 +*
SyntaxError: invalid syntax
>>>
```

Will generate a syntax error, I'll use Backus-Naur Form to explain why we get a syntax error for the example above.

The grammar of almost all programming languages is described in **Backus-Naur Form (BNF).** BNF was developed by John Backus in the 1950s; He was very influential in developing the FORTRAN programming language. The purpose of BNF is to develop a concise way of describing a programming language. The structure BNF is

```
<non-terminal> → replacement
```

The replacement can be replaced with zero or more non-terminal or terminal
Terminals terminate the statement; once it is used it cannot be replaced.

The grammar for mathematical statements can be expressed by the following notation.

```
expression → expression operator expression
expression → number
operator → +, -, *, /, %, ...
number → 0, 1, 2, 3, 4, ...
```

You will notice that there are two lines for defining expression. Together we call this a recursive definition. A recursive definition is where we define something in terms of itself, but there is also a known definition called the base case. This qualify expression as a recursive definition seen that the expression can be replaced by an expression and also by number which is a terminal. This is a very powerful concept in computer science, and is used to define and breakdown many large problems.

113

How do we use this grammar?

Suppose we want to generate the expression
12 + 3 * 15   we can use the following steps.

1. Start out with an expression	*Expression*
2. Replace with expression → expression	**expression** *operator expression*
3. Replace expression → number	**number** *operator expression*
4. Replace number → 12	**12** *operator expression*
5. Replace operator → +	*12* **+** *expression*
6. Replace expression → expression operator expression	*12 +* **expression operator expression**
7. Replace expression → number	*12 +* **number** *operator expression*
8. Replace number → 3	*12 +* **3** *operator expression*
9. Replace operator → *	*12 + 3* ***** *expression*
10. Replace expression → number	*12 + 3 ** **number**
11. Replace number → 15	*12 + 3 ** **15**

The replaced is highlighted on the right.

Now let us try to generate 5 + 4 +*

1. Start out with an expression	*Expression*
2. Replace with expression → expression	**expression** *operator expression*
3. Replace expression → number	**number** *operator expression*
4. Replace number → 5	**5** *operator expression*
5. Replace operator → +	*5* **+** *expression*
6. Replace expression → exp op exp	*5 +* **expression operator expression**
7. Replace expression → number	*5 +* **number** *operator expression*
8. Replace number → 4	*5 +* **4** *operator expression*
9. Replace operator → +	*5 + 4* **+** *expression*
10. Error we cannot replace expression→ operator	*5 + 4 +* **SyntaxError**

It turns out that it is impossible to generate ***5 + 4 + **** using the grammar defined above and therefore the interpreter will generate a syntax error when to try to parse the expression.

114

To reduce or eliminate syntax error:

- Ensure that operators are surrounded by operands (python use what is called an infixed notation and therefore operator must be in the middle of the operands

- Ensure that all opening brackets (, {, [have a matching), },]

- Ensure that all opening quotation " or ' have a matching ' or ".

- Ensure that you include a colon : at the end of your if statement or other control structures.

- Ensure that you are using the correct operator = means assignment and == is equal to.

- Ensure that you are not trying to use a keyword as a variable name, this will generate a syntax error.

- Ensure that you are using the correct indentation. Python is indent sensitive, typically we indent after a colon : and back to the original alignment afterwards.

10.3   Runtime Errors

Runtime errors are more difficult to spot; largely because the program will run without reporting an error to the user which gives the impression that everything is working well. Runtime errors can happen in a few ways:

- The program runs without output. If this is the case then check to ensure that there is output statement in the code unless the code is a module that will be used for utilities.

- If the program hangs and become inactive. This normally happen when the program enters an indeterminate loop without statements to make the condition false. This was mentioned when I introduced the while loop. If this happens the program will run forever. I'll use an example to illustrate this

```
number = 1
while number<10:
    print("The value of number is ", number)
    # notice that there is no statement to make the condition false
```

Notice that in the body of the while loop there is no statement that will change the value of number and therefore number will always be less than 10, and hence the condition will always be true. If this code snippet was in your code, the error would be clear seen that there is a print statement in the body of the while loop, that will be printing "The value of number is 1", on your screen that therefore we could identify where the error is. Now if there was no print statement, for example the while loop was updating a database, or traversing a list for each iteration then this would become more difficult to identify.

- Runtime error can happen when we have a recursive call that does not "bottom out". We use the term "bottom out" to refer to the situation when either there is no base case or the function will never get to the base case. Let us think about the recursive definition for expression in BNF that was mentioned in the syntax error section. We defined expression as:

    expression → expression operator expression
    expression → number

    If the second statement was absent (*expression → number*) then it would not be possible to get to a situation where we have expression in all terminals (numbers and operators).

    Let us use a recursive definition to define a function called power_number(), that takes two values as input, namely a base and an index.

```
def power_number(base, index):
    if index ==0:
        return 1
    else:
        return base * power_number(base, index-1)
```

The base condition in this situation is to return 1 whenever index is equal to zero. This is consistent with mathematics in that any number raised to the power of zero is equal to 1. Now if this base condition was absent or it was impossible to get to the base condition, then after running for some time the interpreter will return a runtime error, stating that maximum recursion depth exceeded in comparison.

```
def power_number(base, index):
    if index ==15:
        return 1
    else:
        return base * power_number(base, index-1)

print(power_number(4,12))
```

In the example above index will never be equal to 15, seen that index starts at 12 from out print statement and decrease in value.

116

```
ors and Exception/errors.py", line 23, in power_number
    return base * power_number(base, index-1)
  File "C:/Users/Devz/Downloads/Python Book/Python for Key stage 4/Chapter 9 Err
ors and Exception/errors.py", line 23, in power_number
    return base * power_number(base, index-1)
  File "C:/Users/Devz/Downloads/Python Book/Python for Key stage 4/Chapter 9 Err
ors and Exception/errors.py", line 20, in power_number
    if index ==15:
RuntimeError: maximum recursion depth exceeded in comparison
>>>
>>>
```

Whenever you suspect that a recursive definition is not getting to the base case, it is worth using a trace table to go through a simple case, or use print statements to display the value of the variables at strategic locations in the function call.

10.4   Semantic or logical Error

Semantic refers to the meaning of a language or logic. Semantic errors are even more difficult to spot than runtime error. Similar to runtime error the interpreter will not give you any message or warning. The program will even run without hanging, or even a maximum recursion depth message. Instead the output will not be the one that you are expecting.

Fortunately there are strategies available to the programmer to identify and correct semantic errors.

- Inserting print() statement at strategic location in your code to see the values of variables is quite helpful.
- The use of trace table to record the value of variables can be also helpful.
- Sometimes it is worth breaking down complex expressions into simpler statements, than having large complex statements.

    If you define a function called larger() that takes two numbers and return the larger of the two. It is possible to use `larger(num1, larger(num2,num3))`, to return the larger of three numbers. That is equivalent to
    `temp_num = larger(num1, num2)`
    `larger(temp_num, num3)`

    This may seem trivial, but it turns out that it is less likely to make mistakes on simpler expressions than complex ones.

- Semantic errors often arise from the use of incorrect operators, for example using the < sign instead of the >.
- It is often worth using brackets to explicitly force the correct order of operation, from our example in the table above

    In evaluating $\frac{15}{2\pi}$ in python we would type `15/2*math.pi`

    Seen that division and multiplication have the same precedence we would get 23.56, instead of the correct answer 2.38. In order to get the correct answer we would have to use brackets therefore, we would type `15/ (2*math.pi)`

10.5 Dealing with errors

Even with the best intention there will be situations in which errors occur in a program that were not foreseen. Many programming languages provide error handing facility for situations like this. In python all exceptions are instance of the baseException class and are implemented using the try statement. The debugger tool in python is called the python debugger and is imported using the `import pdb`. There are two versions of the try statement, namely try-except and try-finally.

10.5.1 The try statement

syntax
```
try:
<block_to_execute>

except <exception>:
    <block_to_execute>
```

Where `<block_to_execute>` is the originally intended code.
`except` must include at least one exception, but can include as many.

Example:

```
try:
    x=int(input("Enter a number to divide: "))
    y=int(input("Enter a number to divide by: "))
    print(x/y)
except ZeroDivisionError:
        print("Cannot divide by zero: ")
        y=1
```

This will catch the exception print a more meaningful statement and continue with the execution of the program.

In the example above the interpreter will try to execute all the statements in the try block. If the user enters zero for the y value, the ZeroDivisionError exception will be raised, instead of halting the program, the interpreter will catch the exception in the "except" clause and recover from the unstable state by re-assigning y to 1. We could have included other exceptions in the "except" clause, and the interpreter would have search until it finds a matching exception to enter into the "except" clause. If no matching exception is found the program will halt/stop and print the exception to the screen.

The example below shows how we can catch an importError (import a file/module that does not exist).

```
>>> import unknown_module
Traceback (most recent call last):
  File "<pyshell#60>", line 1, in <module>
    import unknown_module
ImportError: No module named 'unknown_module'
```

This is the import statement without the exception handler. Note that this would stop the running program. Where as

```
>>> try:
        import unknow_module
except ImportError:
        print("Sorry module not found")


Sorry module not found
>>>
```

With the exception handler the program will recover and continue to run.

10.5.2   The try statement with multiple exceptions

There are situations in which more than one exception can occur in a particular code. You have the option of writing multiple except clauses, where you check each exception and resolve it or you can use one except clause where the interpreter will check through a list of exceptions. It turns out that if there is one way to deal with all exceptions then the later is a better option, but if each exception requires a separate solution then having multiple except clause is the better solution.

If we are writing a program and where we want the user to enter a number then carryout some mathematical operation on this number, we will use the int() function to convert the data entered to an integer. There are two possible exceptions that can occur in this situation, namely:

TypeError: *When an operation or function is attempted that is invalid for the specified data type*
ValueError: *values have the valid type of arguments, but the arguments have invalid values specified.*

The code below will catch both the ValueError and TypeError exception and will print the associated message. In the situation where the course of action is dependent on the type of error, then the solution below is applicable.

```
try:
    x=int(input("Enter a number: "))
except ValueError:
    print("You entered an incorrect value: ")
except TypeError:
    print("The data type is invalid ")

print("Continuing after the input ...")
```

10.5.3 The optional else clause

The optional else clause is used when you only want to execute statements if no exceptions were raised in the try clause.

```
try:
    x=int(input("Enter a number: "))
except (ValueError, TypeError):
    print("Something went wrong")
else:
    print("Nothing went wrong")
```

Notice that if the users input is valid then python will execute the else clause. Notice also that in the code snippet above we have changed from using multiple except clauses to a single one with multiple exceptions (ValueError and TypeError).

10.5.4 The try – finally statement

If we have multiple statements in the try block and one of the statement raises an exception before the end of the try block then the other statements in the try block will be executed. There are situations in which you want the entire try block to be executed even if an exception was raised. It turns out that the try finally statement will resolve this.

syntax

```
try:
    <block_to_execute>

finally:
    <finally_block>
```

Where `<block_to_execute>` is the originally intended code.
  `finally` must block that will be executed regardless of any exception

120

Example:

If we are writing a program that opens a file and do some calculations then close the file. It is a good idea to raise an exception after attempting to open the file. If an error occurs while trying to open the file then the IOError exception is raised. Consider the code below.

```python
try:
    test_file = open("example_file.txt", 'w')
    test_file.write("Some operations")
except IOError:
    print("File don't exist ...")
    test_file.close()
```

If we encounter an error while trying to write to the file, the IOError exception will be raised; the "except" clause will handle the exception and close the file. If no exception is raised then the file will remain open, which is not good for our program. It turns out that the "try finally" can help to solve this problem. Whenever we use the "try finally" statement if an exception is raised, then execution is passed to the finally clause and then to the exception handler in the "except" section. The code snippet below gives this solution.

```python
try:
    test_file = open("example_file.txt", 'w')
    try:
        test_file.write("Some operations")
    finally:
        test_file.close()
except IOError:
    print("File don't exist ...")
```

Notice that if the write statement fails then the file will be closed.

Practice Exercise 10

1. What is a syntax error?

2. Why are semantic or logical errors hard to spot?

3. What kind of error is in the code below?

    ```
    def factorial(num):
        if num ==1:
            return 1
        else:
            return num * factorial(num)
    ```

4. Correct the error in the function above so that it calculates the factorial of a given number. Factorial of n is $n*(n-1)*(n-2)*(n-3)* \ldots 1$.

5. What type of error is in the code below?

    ```
    number = 1
    while number< 13:
        print(number, " Squared is ", number*number)
    ```

6. Correct the error so that the code prints the square numbers from 1 to 12.

7. Use the grammar below to show how the interpreter parse the expression *8*2/1*

    a. expression → expression operator expression
    b. expression → number
    c. operator → +, -, *, /, %, ...
    d. number → 0, 1, 2, 3, 4, ...

8. Re-write the code below, so that if there are no exception while opening and writing to the file, then the file should close, after the update

    ```
    try:
        test_file = open("new_file.txt", 'w')
        test_file.write("Some operations")
    except IOError:
        print("File don't exist ...")
        test_file.close()
    ```

122

Worked Solution

Decorating Company

John a local decorator in your community has approached you to keep track and cost of his jobs. He lays carpets for customers. He has to give his customers accurate quotes, after taking measurements. You are required to develop a computer system that will help him to do this.

Carpets

When a room measurement is taken, the length and the width are taken to find the area as carpet is sold in square meters. He also supplies underlay to go under the carpet and gripper to run along the edge of the carpet to hold the carpet in place. The underlay required is the same amount of carpet required. Seen that the gripper goes around the edge of the carpet; the length of gripper required is the perimeter of the carpet.

Some rooms have bay windows, fireplace and other obstacles, therefore John has to cut the carpet before laying, This does not reduce the price of the carpet. The table below shows how price structure.

Item	Price
Carpets	£22.50 per square meter
Underlay – First Step	£5.99 per square meter
Underlay – Monarch	£7.99 per square meter
Underlay – Royal	£60 per square meter
Gripper	£1.10 per meter

In addition to the raw material, John charges 65 for each hour worked. John charges £65 as a minimum for all jobs. He estimates that it requires an hour for each 16 square meters, this is therefore calculated once the amount goes above 16 square meters.

The system should allow the user to:

1. Enter the customers details
2. List all customers in the system – from this list you should have the ability to add new, delete a customer, or view a quote linked to a selected customer.
3. Add a new quote
4. List all quotation – with an itemized list of the material, and labour cost for each job
5. Save customers and quotation details to an external file

Your each customer the system should save:

- First and surname
- Town
- Telephone number

Each quote consist of

- A customer – The system should be able to add a new customer or select existing customer when creating a quote
- The dimensions of the room (length, width)
- Select the type of underlay
- Calculate the overall cost

Develop the part of the system that allows the user to save a quotation for later use.

Solution

The solution uses the List data structure extensively and uses class to store customer and quotation details. For the control assessment you will need to show more in your solution, in particular you will need to show:

- Explanation of the problem – to demonstrate that you understand the problem that you are going to solve.
- Plan
- Proposed solution – pseudo code or flowchart
- Solution development with annotated code

The solution below is a basic solution with some important features missing, in particular:

- There is no error detection and correction present. The solution assumes that the user will enter the correct data at all times. In particular when the user is prompted for a number, it is assumed that a number will be entered and nothing else. This needs to be more robust for the actual control assessment.
- There is not data validation, for example in entering length, and width, a positive number could be validated.
- Whereas List is a fast effective way of storing and accessing data in the computer's memory in real life, it would be more realistic to save the details (customers, quotation) to a database for more persistent use of data.
- Whereas the solution is meeting the client's need, it would be a better solution to store data such as the price in an external file so that the client can change the price from time to time.

Alternate solutions to this problem can be found on the companion website **http://www.gcsepython.com**

A Possible Solution

The Customer Class

```python
class customer():
    '''
    The customer class, storing the information for each customer:
    firstname, surname, town, address
    '''

    def __init__(self, firstname="First name", surname="surname", town="Town", telephone="070 000 0000"):
        self.firstname=firstname
        self.surname = surname
        self.town = town
        self.telephone = telephone

    def get_firstname(self):
        return self.firstname

    def get_surname(self):
        return self.surname

    def get_town(self):
        return self.town

    def get_telephone(self):
        return self.telephone

    def print_customer(self):
        print("Name is   : ", self.firstname, self.surname)
        print("Town is   : ", self.town)
        print("Telephone: ", self.telephone)

    def set_firstname(self, new_name):
        self.firstname = new_name

    def set_surname(self, new_surname):
        self.surname = new_surname

    def set_town(self, new_town):
        self.town = new_town

    def set_telephone(self, new_telephone):
        self.telephone = new_telephone
```

The Quotation Class

```python
from customer import customer

class quotation():
    '''
    Quotation is  class that stores the information for a quotation, each quote has
    a customer, quotation date, which is input automatically on creation
    dimensions (length and width), underlay_name. length of gripper,
    underlay_price, which is calculated based on underlay selected, and finally
```

```
        the total price.
        '''
    def __init__(self, customer, date, length, width, uname, gripper ):
        '''
        Constructor for quote.
        '''
        self.customer = customer
        self.quotation_date = date
        self.length=length
        self.width = width
        self.underlay_name = uname
        self.gripper = gripper
        self.underlay_price = self.set_underlay_price()
        self.total_price = self.set_total_price()

    def get_customer(self):
        return self.customer

    def get_quotation_date(self):
        return self.quotation_date

    def get_length(self):
        return self.length

    def get_width(self):
        return self.width

    def get_underlay_name(self):
        return self.underlay_name

    def get_underlay_price(self):
        return self.underlay_price

    def get_total_price(self):
        return self.total_price

    def get_gripper(self):
        return self.gripper

    #the print_quotation is used extensively to display the contents of the quote
    def print_quotation(self):
        print("Quotation Details ")
        print(self.customer.print_customer())
        print("Quotation date", self.quotation_date.day, "-",
              self.quotation_date.month, "-", self.quotation_date.year )
        print("Room measurement--> Length:", self.get_length(),
 "Width:",self.get_width(), "Area -->",
              self.get_length()*self.get_width(),"sq. mts")
        print("Underlay",self.get_underlay_name())
        print("Underlay price", self.get_underlay_price())
        print("Total Price ", self.get_total_price())

    #Total price calculated to include cost for material, and labour cost
    def set_total_price(self):
        area = self.length*self.width
        if area >=16:
            labour_cost = (area/16) *65
        else:
```

```python
            labour_cost = 65
        return (area*22.5)+(area*self.get_underlay_price())+labour_cost
    def set_underlay_price(self):
        if self.get_underlay_name() == "First Step":
            return 5.99
        else:
            if self.get_underlay_name() == "Monarch":
                return 7.99
            else:
                if self.get_underlay_name() == "Royal":
                    return 60
                else:
                    return 0

    def set_customer(self, new_customer):
        self.customer = new_customer

    def set_quotation_date(self, new_date):
        self.quotation_date = new_date

    def set_length(self, new_length):
        self.length = new_length

    def set_width(self, new_width):
        self.width = new_width

    def set_underlay_name(self, new_underlay_name):
        self.underlay_name = new_underlay_name
```

The Decorator's Driver File

```python
from customer import customer
from quote import quotation
from datetime import datetime
import sys

customer_list = []
quotation_list = []

# main menu
def main_menu():
    print("Welcome to John's Decorating")
    print("You have the following options:\n")
    print("1)    Add a new customer")
    print("2)    List all customer")
    print("3)    Add a new quote")
    print("4)    List all Quotation")
    print("5)    Save customer details")
    print("6)    Save Quotation to file\n")
    print("0)    Exit")


    choice = int(input("Select one --> "))
    if choice == 1:
        add_customer()
    if choice ==2:
        list_all_customer()
```

```
        if choice ==3:
            add_a_quote()
        if choice ==4:
            list_all_quotations()
        if choice ==5:
            save_customer_details()
        if choice ==6:
            save_quotation()

        if choice ==0:
            print("Good bye ...............")
            sys.exit()

def save_quotation():
    print("Saving Quotations ...")
    file_name=input("Enter the file name to save in : ")
    file_name = file_name+"_quotations.txt"
    quote_file = open(file_name,'w')
    for quote in quotation_list:
        quote_file.write(quote.customer.get_firstname()+"\n")
        quote_file.write(str(quote.get_quotation_date())+ "\n")
        quote_file.write(str(quote.get_length())+ "\n")
        quote_file.write(str(quote.get_width())+ "\n")
        quote_file.write(quote.get_underlay_name()+ "\n")
        quote_file.write(str(quote.get_gripper())+ "\n")
        quote_file.write(str(quote.get_underlay_price())+ "\n")
        quote_file.write(str(quote.get_total_price())+ "\n")
    quote_file.close()

    print("File saved")
    main_menu()

#function used to save customers details
def save_customer_details():
    print("Saving Customers' Details ...")
    file_name=input("Enter the file name to save in : ")
    file_name = file_name+"_customers.txt"
    cust_file = open(file_name,'w')
    for cust in customer_list:
        cust_file.write(cust.get_firstname()+"\n")
        cust_file.write(cust.get_surname()+ "\n")
        cust_file.write(cust.get_town()+ "\n")
        cust_file.write(cust.get_telephone()+ "\n")
    cust_file.close()

    print("File saved")
    main_menu()

#function used to add a new customer, once confirmed save the customer in a
#customer list
def add_customer():
    print("Add customer")
    firstname = input("Enter the customer's first name: ")
    surname = input("Enter the customer's surname:   ")
    town=input("Enter the customer's town: ")
    telephone = input("Please enter the customer's telephone number: ")
    customer1 = customer(firstname, surname,town, telephone)
    customer1.print_customer()
```

```python
        customer_list.append(customer1)
        print("Customer added successfully ...")
        another = input("Would you like to add another? yes [y]  or no [n] --> ")
        if another=='y':
            add_customer()
        else:
            main_menu()

#list all the quotation in the system
def list_all_quotations():
    number =1
    for quote in quotation_list:
        print("Quotation " , str(number))
        quote.print_quotation()
        number = number +1
        print("\n")

    print("[A] Add new     [D] Delete      [B] Back")
    choice=input("-->")
    if choice=='a' or choice=='A':
        add_a_quote()
    else:
        if choice=='d' or choice=='D':
            print("Enter the quotation number to delete")
            quote_num = int(input("--> "))
            quote = quotation_list[quote_num-1]
            print("Are you sure you want to delete: ")
            quote.print_quotation()
            choice = input("[Y] Yes    [N] No")
            if choice =='y' or choice =='Y':
                quotation_list.remove(quote)
                print("Quotation removed ")
                main_menu()
            else:
                list_all_quotations()
        else:
            main_menu()

def list_all_customer():
    number =1
    for cust in customer_list:
        print("Customer" , str(number))
        cust.print_customer()
        number = number +1
        print("\n")

    print("[A] Add new     [D] Delete    [V] View Quote for customer      [B] Back")
    choice = input("What would you like to do --> ")
    if choice == 'a' or choice=='A':
        add_customer()
    else:
        if choice =='d' or choice =='D':
            delete_customer()
        else:
            if choice ==  'v' or choice =="V":
                view_quote()
            else:
                main_menu()
```

```python
def add_a_quote():
    print("Add new Quote")
    print("[N] New customer        [E] Exiting customer")
    choice=input("-->")
    if choice == 'n' or choice == 'N':
        customer1 = add_customer_for_quote()
    else:
        customer1 = search_for_existing_customer()

    length = int(input("Enter the Length: "))
    width = int(input("Enter the width: "))
    print("Underlay Choice")
    print("[F] First Step (5.99)    [M] Monarch (7.99)       [R] Royal (60)")
    choice=input("-->")
    if choice == 'f' or choice =='F':
        uname = "First Step"
    else:
        if choice =='m' or choice =='M':
            uname="Monarch"
        else:
            uname="Royal"
    gripper = 2*length + 2*width
    quotation1 = quotation(customer1, datetime.now(), length, width, uname, gripper)
    quotation1.print_quotation()
    print("[A] Add    [D] Delete")
    choice=input("-->")
    if choice=='a' or choice =='A':
        quotation_list.append(quotation1)
        print("Quote added successfully")
        main_menu()
    else:
        main_menu()

def add_customer_for_quote():
    print("Add customer For new Quote")
    firstname = input("Enter the customer's first name: ")
    surname = input("Enter the customer's surname:   ")
    town=input("Enter the customer's town: ")
    telephone = input("Please enter the customer's telephone number: ")
    customer1 = customer(firstname, surname,town, telephone)
    #customer1.print_customer()
    customer_list.append(customer1)
    return customer1

def search_for_existing_customer():
    number =1
    print("Here is a list of all customers ")
    for cust in customer_list:
        print("Customer" , str(number))
        cust.print_customer()
        number = number +1
        print("\n")
    print("enter the customer number to add a quote for ")
    cust_number=int(input("-->"))
    customer1=customer_list[cust_number-1]
    return customer1
```

```python
def delete_customer():
    print("Delete Customer")
    cust_number=int(input("Enter the customer number to delete --> "))
    customer1 = customer_list[cust_number-1]
    print("Customer")
    customer1.print_customer()
    print("Are you sure you want to delete [Y] Yes     [N] No")
    choice = input("--> ")
    if choice =='y' or choice=='Y':
        customer_list.remove(customer1)
        print("Customer information Deleted  ...")
    main_menu()

def view_quote():
    print("View Quote")
    print("Enter the customer's number to view quote")
    choice = int(input("-->"))
    customer1=customer_list[choice-1]

    #Create a dummy quote, just in case the customer do not have a quote saved
    target_quote = quotation(customer1, datetime.now(), 0, 0, "dummy", 0 )
    #Now search for the quotation with the customer
    for quote in quotation_list:
        if quote.customer == customer1:
            target_quote = quote
    if target_quote.get_underlay_name() == "dummy":
        print("Sorry", customer1.get_firstname(), "does not have a quote ")
        print("Here is a list of all your customers")
        list_all_customer()
    else:
        target_quote.print_quotation()
        choice=input("continue --> ")
        main_menu()

main_menu()
```

Quick How To

Task	How To
Append an element to a list	`List_name.append(element)`

Clear the screen	`import os   #first import the os library`
	
	`os.system('cls')`

Close an open file	`File_handler.close()`

Define a initialize a class with default values	`def __init__(self,value1=<default1>, value2 = <default2>):`
	`    self.value1 = value1`
	`    self.value2 = value2`

Declare an empty list	`List_name = []`
Empty a Dictionary	`if len(dictionary_name)>0:` `    dictionary_name.clear()`
Empty a List	`if len(list_name)>0:` `    del list_name[:]`
Import a library	`from datetime import datetime` `import sys`
Increment a variable	`variable_name = variable_name +1`
Open a file for reading	`text_file = open(file_name, "r")`

Use a docstring in a class	`'''`
	`    This is a docstring, to include information about the class`
	`'''`

Glossary

Word	Meaning
Absolute path	A path that gives the specific location on a file system regardless of where the address is given from. This should contain the root directory and all other sub-directories to get to a file.
Algorithm	A collection of unambiguous and executable operations to perform some task in a finite amount of time
Abstract Data Type (ADT)	These are new data types that numerous operations defined on.
Argument	These are the actual values that are supplied during the function call. The arguments are then matched with the parameter in the function prototype.
Attributes	Data items that an object possess.
Boolean	This is a data type having two values usually denoted true or false.
Built-in Function	These are functions made within an application and can be accessed by the end users.
Calculation	Any mathematical operations done on numbers
Class	It is a user defined data type that is made up of attributes and methods. (These are known as ADT)
Compilers	These create object codes which are passed on to the executers to be interpreted
Computer Science	The study of the design of algorithms, their properties, linguistic and mechanical realisation
Control Structures	Blocks of codes that dictate the flow of control within a program
Database	This is a collection of tables that store data.
Data Encapsulation	This is information hiding. It involves reusing codes in a previously defined class. The user does not have to know the attributes or methods of the defined class
Data types	The range of value that can be stored and the kind of operations (addition, subtraction, comparison, concatenation, etc) that are possible on a given variable.
DBMS	Database Management System- software used to arrange tables in a systematic manner.
Directory Structure	is the way in which an operating system displays its files to the user
Exception	This is when an error occurs in a program. This can be a programmer's or

Word	Meaning
	a software error.
Expressions	A combination of operator and operations that evaluate to a value.
Float	A data type made up of numbers that has a decimal place
Function	These are a block of codes that perform a specific task
Integer	This is a data type made up of any positive or negative whole number.
Interactive Mode	A mode in python where instructions are typed at the python prompt and individual line of instruction is executed at a time.
Interpreters	These take each line, translate and execute the translated line, before turning its attention to the other line.
List	This is a mutable collection of data items, which can be of the same or different data types.
Object	This is a thing or an event in our application
Object –Oriented Programming	A type of programming that defines the data type and functions of a data structure
Parameter	These are the place holders that are used in defining the function prototype.
Program code	The set of instructions normally written in high-level programming language that the computer follow to complete a task.
Programming Paradigm	Different disciplines and principles involve in programming
Python	Python is an interpreted general purpose programming language which conforms to multiple ways of programming
Query	A question that is asked of the database.
Quotient	This is the number of times one quantity can be divided by another quantity. It is the result of a division.
Recursive	A rule or a procedure that can be applied repeatedly.
Relative path	This starts the path by using the current directory.
Run-time error	Error occurs during execution of a program.
Script	A program that is normally interpreted stored as a file
Semantics	Error in logics of the program. It encompasses the meaning of the program and its output.
SQL	Structured Query Language- the universal language used to create and manipulate databases.

Word	Meaning
Statements	This is used to store the value of an expression in a variable
String	This a data type made up of characters. These can be letters, numbers and symbols
Syntax	Error of language, usually the code does not conform to the grammar of the language
Values	Any literal that can be stored in a memory location
Variables	A named memory location

References

Aitel David, Diamond Jason, Foster-Johnson Eric, Norton Peter, Parker Aleatha, Richardson Leonard, Roberts Michael, Samuel Alex (2005), "Beginning Python", Wiley Publishing Inc. Indianapolis, Indiana.

Allen Downey (2008), "Think Python, How to think like a Computer Scientist", Green Tea Press.

Hetland Magnus Lie (2005), "Beginning Python , From Novice to Professional", Apress.

Gupta Rashi (2002), "Making use of Python", Wiley Publishing Inc. New York.

Printed in Great Britain
by Amazon.co.uk, Ltd.,
Marston Gate.